Also available from the American Academy of Pediatrics

Caring for Your Baby and Young Child
Birth to Age 5

El Cuidado De Su Hijo Pequeño
Desde Que Nace Hasta Los Cinco Años

Caring for Your School-Age Child
Ages 5 to 12

Caring for Your Teenager

Your Baby's First Year

El Primer Año De Su Bebé

Guide to Your Child's Symptoms
Birth Through Adolescence

Guide to Your Child's Sleep
Birth Through Adolescence

Guide to Your Child's Allergies and Asthma
Breathing Easy and Bringing Up Healthy, Active Children

Guide to Your Child's Nutrition
Making Peace at the Table and Building Healthy Eating Habits for Life

New Mother's Guide to Breastfeeding

Nueva Guía De Lactancia Materna

Guide to Toilet Training

Guía Para Enseñar Al Niño A Usar El Inodoro

ADHD: A Complete and Authoritative Guide

Baby & Child Health: The Essential Guide From Birth to 11 Years

For bedwetting updates and
related information, please visit
Dr Bennett's Web site,
www.wakingupdry.com.

Waking Up Dry

A Guide to Help Children Overcome Bedwetting

HOWARD J. BENNETT, MD, FAAP

American Academy of Pediatrics
DEDICATED TO THE HEALTH OF ALL CHILDREN™

American Academy of Pediatrics
Department of Marketing and Publications Staff

Maureen DeRosa, MPA
Director, Department of Marketing and Publications

Mark Grimes
Director, Division of Product Development

Eileen Glasstetter, MS
Manager, Consumer Publishing

Sandi King, MS
Director, Division of Publishing and Production Services

Theresa Wiener
Manager, Editorial Production

Kate Larson
Manager, Editorial Services

Jason Crase
Editorial Specialist

Peg Mulcahy
Graphic Designer

Jill Ferguson
Director, Division of Marketing and Sales

Linda Smessaert
Manager, Publication and Program Marketing

Library of Congress Control Number: 2004111853
ISBN: 1-58110-156-2
CB0036

Cover photography by Patricia Mathes Lake
Illustrations by John Regnier and Peg Mulcahy

The recommendations in this publication do not indicate an exclusive course of treatment or serve as a standard of medical care. Variations, taking into account individual circumstances, may be appropriate.

Products are mentioned for informational purposes only. Inclusion in this publication does not imply an endorsement by the American Academy of Pediatrics.

9-127/0505

For my patients, who taught me about
bedwetting as I developed this program.

Acknowledgments

Although this book is a written account of my Waking Up Dry
Program, a number of people helped it grow from a clinical protocol
to an actual book. First, I would like to thank Monica Adler for
suggesting that I "take my show on the road." Without her enthusiasm and good-natured prodding, this book would never have
been written. I would also like to thank the following friends and
colleagues who reviewed the manuscript: Linda Goldstein, MD,
FAAP; Inas Anderson, MD, FAAP; Barry Belman, MD, FAAP; Dale
Gertz, MD, FAAP; William Hulbert, MD, FAAP; and Mandy Katz.
Debbie Gilbert, MLS, AHIP, was instrumental in helping me track
down references I needed to review. I got some additional help
from William S. Haubrich, MD, and Angie Cheek, VMD, who
provided information I needed for some of the filler I used in the
book. I would also like to thank my wife Jan, who not only picked
up the slack whenever I disappeared into the basement to work
on the book, but also provided terrific insight when she read the
manuscript in its earliest stages.

Because no one practices medicine in a vacuum, I would like
to thank my clinical teachers and all of the people who have
conducted research on bedwetting. In particular, I would like to
thank Barton Schmitt, MD, FAAP, whose writings on bedwetting
have had a big influence on how I approach the condition.

I am very grateful for everyone at the American Academy of
Pediatrics who helped make this project a reality. Eileen Glasstetter
and Mark Grimes saw the potential in a self-help book that spoke
directly to children. Jason Crase is a copy editor extraordinaire and
Peg Mulcahy did a terrific job giving the book an appealing look that
children will appreciate.

Contents

Introduction for Kids

Your parents bought this book because they want to help you become dry at night. I'm a pediatrician (a kid's doctor), and I've been helping children overcome bedwetting for 25 years. This book describes the program I use with patients in my office. I wrote the book because my Waking Up Dry Program really works, and a number of parents and doctor friends encouraged me to write about what I do.

Bedwetting is not a serious medical condition, but it can be very difficult to live with. Wetting at night makes it hard to go on sleepovers; it makes you feel uncomfortable in the morning; and worst of all, it's upsetting not to have control over your own body while you sleep. But the good news is that you can do something about it. With motivation and practice, you can become the boss of your body! (*Motivation* means that you want something enough to work for it.)

If you tried to stop bedwetting in the past and it didn't work, I can understand that you might not want to try something new. The main reason programs fail is because children don't get enough support to make it through the rough spots. The Waking Up Dry Program has a winning record for 3 reasons. First, it's filled with lots of tips that help you along the way. Second, the program attacks the problem from different angles. Third—and most important—it lets you play a big role in setting up and carrying out the program.

When I work with children in my office, I talk to them as much as their parents. In the same way, I will be talking to you throughout the book. I will also be giving your parents special instructions along the way because we need their help to make the program work. In my office, I tell kids that I will be their coach and their parents will be my assistant coaches. You are the player! You are the star! But you will also be the one who does most of the work. One of the things I will say over and over is how important it is for you to be involved with the program. Whether it's filling out your Waking Up Dry Calendar or cooperating with your coaches, the more motivated you are, the more likely it is that you will become dry. Because I wrote the book for children of different ages, you may need your coach (mom or dad) to read the book to you. That's okay. That's one of the things coaches do. In fact, they need to read the book *with you* even if they don't need to read the book *to you*. Some of the information in the book is complicated, even for good readers, and going through it with your coaches will improve your chances of becoming dry. Also, your coaches need to help out with many parts of the program. Together, all of us will work really hard so you can start waking up every morning in a nice dry bed.

Finally, I want you to know that I love being a pediatrician, and one of my greatest joys as a doctor is helping kids become dry at night. So even though I won't become your personal doctor, I hope my book will help you beat bedwetting forever!

Dr B

Introduction for Parents

It's been known for a long time that bedwetting resolves on its own in most cases. Every year, 15% of children who wet the bed become dry without any intervention. This fact has led many doctors to simply reassure patients that the condition is not serious and that it will go away on its own. The problem with this approach is that bedwetting can affect a child's self-esteem. Therefore, it's short-sighted to ask a child to wait years to become dry if treatment can expedite the process. On the other hand, given the rate of spontaneous improvement, you should always consider 2 things before starting any treatment: (1) Is your child motivated to become dry? (2) Is the treatment safe?

Some doctors prescribe medication to stop bedwetting. Although medication may be helpful, it doesn't cure the problem, and one of the drugs used to treat bedwetting (imipramine) has potentially serious side effects. Many doctors appropriately inform parents about behavior management techniques (including a special device called the bedwetting alarm), which are the most effective treatments for bedwetting. Unfortunately, exploring the many facets of treatment is difficult to accomplish during routine checkups, and doctors often don't have the time needed to do this. For example, although bedwetting alarms come with instructions, a child's chances of becoming dry increase dramatically if an experienced practitioner helps her avoid the pitfalls associated with treatment. The information in this book is designed to provide that guidance.

There are a few things you should know right away.

- While much of the book is directed to children, you are an essential part of the program. (Even highly motivated children need their parents' assistance to make the program work.)

- Bedwetting is not your fault. You will learn more about the causes of bedwetting in Chapter 3, but for now, let go of any guilt you've been carrying around for the past few years.

- Bedwetting is not your child's fault, either. No one wets the bed on purpose. However, because bedwetting is draining both physically and emotionally, many parents feel some degree of frustration, helplessness, and anger when they have to deal with wet beds day after day.

- It's important that you present a positive attitude to your child throughout the program because negative emotions undermine what we're trying to accomplish. (Even subtle signs of disapproval can result in more wetting.) Think of yourself as a soccer coach who always says something uplifting, even when a player stumbles and misses the ball. "Great effort, Alex, I know you'll whack it next time!"

- It's equally important that you are prepared to do the program. Teaching children to be dry means extra laundry, having to coax and support them when they're frustrated, and negotiating with your spouse over who's helping with which part of the program. If your child uses the bedwetting alarm, it also means having to deal with fatigue because the alarm wakes you up at night.

- Despite these challenges, helping your child become dry can be one of the most gratifying experiences you will have as a parent!

In Chapter 6, I give children an assignment to find out how motivated they are to become dry at night. Right now, I'd like to be more philosophical about the issue of readiness. Consciously or otherwise, society puts pressure on parents for their children to achieve developmental goals at specific times. Most of us have worried about our children because they were a little "late" with one skill or another. Because evaluating a child's development is a big part of general pediatrics, I spend a lot of time reassuring parents that their children are normal and recommending that we give them time to develop at their own pace.

T. Berry Brazelton, MD, FAAP, was one of the first pediatricians to call for a child-oriented approach to toilet training and bladder control, and those same principles should be applied to the Waking Up Dry Program. Dr Brazelton told parents 40 years ago to hold off on potty training until the child showed signs that she was ready. If parents waited for these cues, toileting usually proceeded smoothly. If they didn't, the process was prolonged or they ran into difficulty.

Although there is no magic age when children are ready to work on their wetting, most children show some awareness of the problem by the time they are 5 to 6 years old. (This is the age when children realize that their friends are no longer wearing Pull-Ups to bed.) Whether children say anything about this depends on their personalities and how they approach learning new skills. Some children communicate their worries directly. Others keep things to themselves or, paradoxically, overcompensate by acting out. If your child has said something to you about wanting to be dry, it's appropriate to use the book. If your child is oblivious about her wetting, you can read the book yourself so you're prepared to deal with the situation once she does become ready. (There is a lot of practical advice in the book, which will make living with bedwetting easier.) If you sense that your child wants to be dry, but she hasn't said anything about it, you can explore this area to see if your hunch is correct. The best time to talk with your child is when she is well rested, well fed, and free of distractions. If your child responds positively to these queries, you can use the book. If she doesn't, put it away for a while, but keep your radar turned on for signs that she has changed her mind. The following are some ways to find out if your child is interested in becoming dry:

- Ask your child if there is anything about being wet (or wearing Pull-Ups) that she doesn't like.

- Ask your child if she would like to stop wearing Pull-Ups.

- Ask your child if she would like to be dry at night.

- If you or a relative wet the bed as kids, share this information with your child so she knows that someone else in the family had the same problem she does. You can help children talk about their feelings if you go first. "When I was your age, I hated waking up in a wet bed."

- Tell your child that you bought a book that teaches kids how to be dry at night. Let her know that the book is fun to read and it will show her how to be the boss of her body.

Finally, please note that the book is not meant to treat children with complicated forms of bedwetting. While most children with nighttime wetting do not have a medical condition that underlies the problem, it's important to exclude such possibilities before you start the program (see Chapter 4).

Howard Bennett, MD, FAAP

How to Use the Book

It's normal for kids to want to jump into the program right after they get the book. Although I know you're eager to start, it's important to read the book from the beginning. The reason for this is that some of the things at the end of the book build on information I discuss earlier. There are 2 chapters, however, that you may want to look at right away: "Sleepovers" (Chapter 23) and "What to Do if Someone Discovers Your Supplies" (Chapter 24).

I spent a lot of time thinking about ways to make the book easier to use. One of the ideas I came up with was to highlight certain sections within each chapter. The following guides describe all of the special sections you will see in the book:

 HANDS ON — This refers to activities or simple experiments that you can do to better understand the way your body works.

KID'S ALERT — I placed this heading by parts of the program that you should pay close attention to.

 FUN FACTS — When I researched the book, I found some interesting facts that I wanted to share with you. Although some of them are not directly related to the program, I think you'll enjoy them.

 TIPS & TRICKS — There are lots of practical ideas in the book, both for you and your coaches. I used this heading for certain ones I wanted to bring to your attention.

 Patient's Story — As you read the book, you will see some stories from actual patients of mine. I included these stories to highlight certain points. These are all real people, but the names are made up.

 COACH'S CORNER — This refers to a section at the back of most chapters that's specifically for your coaches.

Because I want to help as many children as possible, I wrote the book so you can do the program at home with your parents. Don't forget, however, that your doctor or nurse practitioner is also interested in your becoming dry. There are 2 advantages to working with a medical professional: (1) we've done this before, and (2) we can sometimes motivate kids better than parents. If you use the book with your doctor or nurse practitioner, he or she may change the program a little. That's okay because we each have our own way of doing things.

Here is a summary of the information you will find in the book:

- **Part 1** describes how many kids wet the bed, how your body works, and why kids are wet at night. It contains a questionnaire to help you figure out the type of wetting you have.

- **Part 2** tests your motivation for becoming dry by having you do the same Dry-Bed Homework I give patients in my office. This consists of 4 tasks: going to the bathroom when you need to, making a calendar to keep track of your wet and dry nights, finding out the size of your bladder, and determining if you can wake up at night to loud sound.

- **Part 3** shows you how to score your Dry-Bed Homework and introduces you to some bladder exercises and other parts of the program.

- **Part 4** describes the bedwetting alarm, which is the most successful tool you can use to become dry at night.

- **Part 5** shows you how to set up the Waking Up Dry Program. It includes a contract that you and your coaches will sign and lots of tips to help you make it through the rough spots.

- **Part 6** includes chapters on sleepovers, what to do if someone finds your bedwetting supplies, and other techniques that can help you stay dry at night.

- **Part 7** is for coaches. It includes tips on dealing with wet beds and information on medicine that some kids need to become dry.

- **The appendices** include additional information for you, your coaches, and your doctor or nurse practitioner.

Oh, I almost forgot. Throughout the book, you will notice a couple of characters hanging around making helpful or silly comments. Bladderman is the one in the official costume and Nephron (NEF-ron) is the one in regular clothes. Bladderman graduated from superhero school years ago. Nephron wants to be a superhero when he grows up, but right now he's working with Bladderman to become dry at night.

COACH'S CORNER

Research has shown that children are more motivated to become dry if they are actively involved with the treatment plan. This gives kids a sense of "ownership" for the program and increases their chances for success. Although *Waking Up Dry* is a parenting book, I want children to see it as *their* book as well. To help accomplish this goal, I organized the book so I am "talking" to them the same way I do with patients in my office. Given the age range of children who wet at night, this proved to be a bit of a challenge—while I did not want to talk down to older kids, I also did not want to overload or confuse younger ones. To make this work, I need your help. If you come across material that looks too complicated for your child, edit or condense what you read to make it easier. This will not only keep your child interested in the book, but it will help him do a better job with the program.

Although becoming dry is everyone's ultimate goal, children have lots of small successes (as well as setbacks) before they complete the program. It's important to praise your child when you notice these gains because it lets him know you're proud of his accomplishments. (It also motivates him to work on the program.) Look for success in the following areas:

- Enthusiasm about the book
- Asking questions about his body or the program
- Cooperation with the program
- Showing responsibility for doing a task
- Carrying out a task properly
- Making gains with any part of the program (eg, filling out his calendar, doing his bladder exercises)
- Waking up to the bedwetting alarm
- Waking up on his own to pee
- Having smaller wet spots
- Having fewer wet episodes per night
- Having dry nights

While there is no set age when children are ready to work on becoming dry, most of the kids I treat are 6 years and older. (Bedwetting is so common that most doctors don't consider it to be a "problem" until children are 6 years of age.) As you read through the book, you may find that your child will do better with a "low-key" approach. This means you can skip the Dry-Bed Homework and stick with the easier aspects of the program (see "Katie's Story" in Chapter 6 on page 43). In addition, Chapter 28 summarizes which parts of the program are appropriate for children according to their ages.

PART 1

Facts About Bedwetting

CHAPTER 1

You Are Not Alone

Michael's Story

Michael is a 9-year-old boy who saw me for a bedwetting visit a few years ago. When I entered the room, Michael was sitting on a chair next to his mom and dad. His arms were folded in his lap and his face was pointed toward the floor.

I knew right away that Michael was embarrassed about coming to see me. I started the visit by asking him lots of questions about school and his favorite hobbies. After a few minutes, Michael brightened up and we started talking about why kids wet at night and what they can do to become dry. When I told Michael how many children wet the bed, his jaw dropped. He couldn't believe it. All these years he thought he was the only one who woke up every morning in a cold, wet bed. As I watched Michael's face, I saw a huge burden melt away like a snowman on a warm afternoon. The rest of the visit sailed by. Michael became dry 4 weeks after he started the program.

One of the first things I tell kids at bedwetting visits is that they are not the only ones who have trouble staying dry at night. Because bedwetting is a private matter, people usually do not talk about it outside the family. As a result, most children (and some parents) think they are the only ones who have the problem. This is not true. Although it's hard to believe, there are more than 5 million children in the United States who wet the bed. I will discuss why this happens in Chapter 3. Right now, I want to give you a sense of how big the number **5 MILLION** really is.

- If 5 million elephants were lined up end to end, they would stretch all the way around the world.
- If you built a tower out of 5 million soccer balls, it would be as tall as the Washington Monument.
- If you invited 5 million children to see a professional baseball game, you would need 100 stadiums to find them all seats.

When I see children at work, they often ask me how many kids their own age wet the bed. The best way to understand these numbers is to figure out how many kids wet the bed in different grades at school. First, we'll look at children in elementary school. Let's say we take a school that has 500 children from kindergarten to fifth grade (this means the school has kids ranging from 5 to 10 years of age). Table 1 shows how many kids wet the bed in each grade.

When you add up these numbers, it turns out that in an elementary school of 500 children, 50 are wet at night!

Table 1
Number of Students Who Wet the Bed in an Elementary School of 500 Children

Grade	Number Who Wet the Bed
Fifth	🚶🚶🚶🚶 (4)
Fourth	🚶🚶🚶🚶🚶 (5)
Third	🚶🚶🚶🚶🚶🚶 (6)
Second	🚶🚶🚶🚶🚶🚶🚶🚶 (8)
First	🚶🚶🚶🚶🚶🚶🚶🚶🚶🚶 (10)
Kindergarten	🚶🚶🚶🚶🚶🚶🚶🚶🚶🚶🚶 🚶🚶🚶🚶🚶 (17)

Krista's Story

A few years ago, I saw a 10-year-old girl for a bedwetting visit. When I told Krista how many kids are wet at night, she did not look relieved. Instead, she focused on the fifth-grade numbers. "You mean there are only 4 kids in my grade who wet the bed?" I told her that was actually a large number, but sensing her disappointment I did some homework. I found out there are approximately 50,000 elementary schools in the United States. If there are 4 fifth graders at each school who wet the bed, that means there are 200,000 fifth graders in the country with the same problem. That number made Krista feel a lot better.

Now let's do the same thing for middle school. Because middle schools are usually bigger than elementary schools, we'll take a school that has 1,000 children from sixth through eighth grade (this means the school has kids ranging from 11 to 13 years of age). Table 2 shows how many kids wet the bed in each grade.

When you add up these numbers, it turns out that in a middle school of 1,000 children, 31 are wet at night!

Now comes the interesting part. When you add up the thousands and thousands of schools in our country, you can see why there are

Table 2
Number of Students Who Wet the Bed in a Middle School of 1,000 Children

Grade	Number Who Wet the Bed
Eighth	🧍🧍🧍🧍🧍🧍🧍🧍 (8)
Seventh	🧍🧍🧍🧍🧍🧍🧍🧍🧍🧍 (10)
Sixth	🧍🧍🧍🧍🧍🧍🧍🧍🧍🧍🧍🧍🧍 (13)

more than 5 million children in the United States who wet the bed at night. **You are not alone!**

COACH'S CORNER

My husband wet the bed until he was 7, but my 9-year-old is still wet at night. When will he become dry?

Every year, 15% of children become dry on their own. Although children usually follow the same pattern as their parents, this is not always the case. Because there is no way to predict when your son will overcome his wetting, I recommend that you start the program if he's motivated to become dry.

My daughter used to wet the bed every night, but now she's dry half the time. What percentage of 11-year-olds are still wet at night?

I always use the school-based statistics with children because those numbers are easier to understand. Table 3 illustrates how many children wet the bed at different ages.

Table 3
Percentage of Children Who Wet the Bed According to Age

Age	Percent Who Are Wet
5-year-olds	20%
6-year-olds	12%
7-year-olds	10%
8-year-olds	7%
9-year-olds	6%
10-year-olds	5%
11-year-olds	4%
12-year-olds	3%
13-year-olds	2.5%
14-year-olds	2%
15-year-olds	1.5%
16-year-olds	1%

CHAPTER 2

How Your Body Works

The title of this chapter is a little misleading. If I taught you how your entire body works, it would take hundreds of pages. Also, because this is a book about becoming dry at night, it wouldn't help much if I discussed how you breathe or why your poop smells bad. So I'll concentrate on something called the *urinary tract* (see Figure 1).

    The urinary tract is the part of the body that makes urine, stores urine, and tells you when it's time to find a bathroom—or a tree if you're in the woods. (*Urine* is the grown-up word for pee.)

Why Do People Make Urine?

Before I answer this, I want to ask you a question. Do you know the name of the smelly gas that comes out of a car's tailpipe when the

Figure 1
Urinary Tract

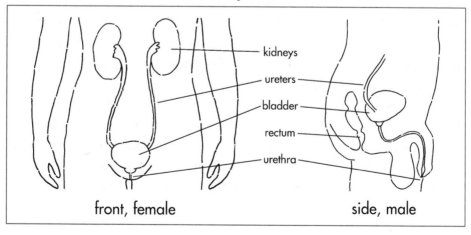

front, female   side, male

kidneys
ureters
bladder
rectum
urethra

engine is running? It's called *exhaust.* Exhaust is a waste product
that an engine produces. It is what's left over after the engine burns
gasoline to make the energy that runs the car. Well, believe it or not,
people are similar to machines. Our bodies are made up of billions
of tiny parts called *cells.* We have many different kinds of cells in
our bodies—muscle cells, brain cells, and skin cells, to name a few.
Each cell has a job. Muscle cells help us move; brain cells help us
think; and skin cells protect us from germs and other things that
can hurt our bodies. Each cell is like a tiny machine, and our cells
need energy to work, just like a car engine needs gasoline to run.
We get this energy from the food we eat, which is why your parents
are always bugging you to eat well.

Anyway, just as a car makes exhaust, our cells produce waste
that the body must get rid of to keep us healthy. The body does this
in many ways, and one of the systems it uses to accomplish this task
is the urinary tract. Some of the waste that our cells make goes into
our blood. The blood is then filtered through our *kidneys,* which
make urine.

How Do the Kidneys Make Urine?

The kidneys are like special filters that remove waste and extra water from the blood. Each kidney has about 1 million tiny filters called *nephrons* (NEF-rons) that do this important work. To remove these waste products, all of the blood in your body passes through your kidneys hundreds of times per day. As the blood passes through each nephron, a tiny amount of urine is made. These tiny drops of urine then pass to a collecting area before draining out of the kidney.

Where Are the Kidneys Located?

Your kidneys are located below your rib cage on each side of your body (you can't feel them because they're way in the back, behind your intestines). Because kidneys are located in the middle of our bodies, we need a way for the urine to get out. Fortunately, our body has an answer for this problem, and it's called the *bladder*.

FUN FACT Your body works hard to keep you healthy even while you're sleeping. During sleep your heart is beating, your lungs are breathing, your intestines are digesting the food you ate for dinner, and your kidneys are filtering your blood to make urine.

What Is the Bladder?

The bladder is a muscular pouch (a balloon made of muscle) that stores urine. It's located about 4 inches below your belly button and is shaped a little like an upside-down triangle. You can find your bladder by putting your hands on your body just above your penis or vagina (no giggling!). If you push down you will feel something hard under your fingers. This is your pubic bone. The bladder is right behind the pubic bone.

SOMETIMES, WHEN YOUR BLADDER IS FULL, YOU CAN PUSH ON YOUR TUMMY AND YOU WILL FEEL LIKE YOU HAVE TO PEE.

How Does the Bladder Work?

After the kidneys make urine, it trickles down to the bladder through 2 tubes called the *ureters* (YUR-ah-ters). As your bladder fills up with urine, it sends a signal to your brain letting you know that it's time to pee. If you're near a bathroom when this happens, you simply go to the toilet and pee. If you can't get to a bathroom right away, you try to hold it for a while. There are 2 things that people do to hold back urine. First, if the urge to pee is mild, your brain tells your bladder to "cool it" and the bladder relaxes so it can hold more urine. Second, if your bladder is too full to relax, you squeeze a special muscle to hold in your urine until you can get to a bathroom. This is called the *sphincter* (sss-FINK-ter) *muscle* (see Figure 2). There's a balloon experiment on page 15 that shows you how this muscle works.

Some children have trouble understanding how their bladders can send a signal to their brains telling them it's time to pee. Most kids realize that they feel a tickle or pressure feeling when they need to go, but the "signal thing" confuses them. The reason the bladder is able to do this is because we have something in our bodies called *nerves*. Nerves are special cells that work like tiny telephone wires sending information from one part of the body to another. Try the experiment on the next page and you'll see what I'm talking about.

Figure 2
Urinary Tract With Sphincter Muscle

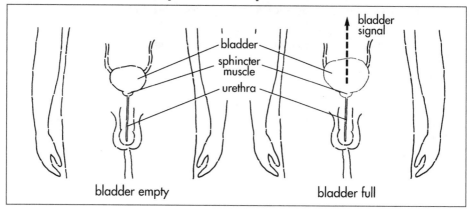

bladder signal

bladder

sphincter muscle

urethra

bladder empty

bladder full

HANDS ON

Sit on a chair and have one of your coaches stand in front of you. Place your hands on your legs and close your eyes. Have your coach gently touch one of your hands. Can you tell which hand is being touched? How can you do that if your eyes are closed? The answer is, you felt it. When your coach touches your hand, the *feeling nerves* in your skin send a signal to your brain telling you that you've been touched. If you didn't have nerves in your skin, you wouldn't know you were being touched. Well, the bladder has special *stretching nerves* inside and when it fills up with urine, these nerves send a signal to your brain telling you that it's time to pee. In most cases, the bladder sends its first signal to the brain when it's half full. As it fills up with more and more urine, the signal gets stronger and stronger, telling your brain that you really need to pee.

FUN FACT

(for boys)

Did your parents ever tell you how much you peed on them when you were a little baby? It usually happened when they changed your diaper. Imagine yourself as a baby, lying on the changing table. After your parents took off your diaper, they probably stood there saying how cute you were, when all of a sudden, WHAMMO! You peed right in their faces. Newborn babies have really small bladders, maybe the size of a large strawberry, and they pee up to 20 times per day. Baby girls pee just as much as boys, but they're less likely to hit someone in the face.

Because your bladder fills up with urine the same way a balloon fills up with water, I've got another experiment to show you. This one can get a little messy, but it's a great way to picture how your bladder works.

HANDS ON

1. Take a medium-sized balloon and attach the open end to a faucet.
2. Turn on the faucet and slowly fill the balloon with water until it's the size of a large orange.
3. Remove the balloon from the faucet, being careful to not spray water all over yourself or your coach.
4. Squeeze the neck of the balloon with your thumb and index finger and turn the balloon upside down. (The neck of the balloon is the thin part that's right behind the opening.)
5. The balloon now looks something like your bladder.
6. Hold the balloon over the sink and relax your thumb and index finger slightly. Water will flow from the opening the same way it comes out of your bladder when you pee.
7. Squeeze the balloon's neck and notice that the water stops coming out. This is the same way your sphincter muscle works. If you squeeze your sphincter muscle while you're peeing, it will stop the stream and keep the rest of the urine in your bladder. If you squeeze your sphincter muscle when your bladder is full, the urine will stay inside.

SQUEEZING YOUR SPHINCTER MUSCLE FEELS THE SAME AS SQUEEZING YOUR "BOTTOM" MUSCLES WHEN YOU'RE TRYING TO HOLD IN A POOP.

How Does Urine Get Out of the Body?

As you can see in figures 1 and 2, urine comes out of your bladder through a tube called the *urethra* (you-REE-thra). In boys, the urethra goes through the penis. In girls, the urethra goes to a small opening right above the vagina. In case you haven't noticed, you don't have to push to get urine out of your body—all you have to do is relax, and your bladder takes care of the rest.

COACH'S CORNER

Why don't children stop playing or watching TV when they need to go to the bathroom?

Parents ask me this question all the time. Although my answer is just a guess, I think children often don't want to bother with the basic needs of their bodies. Toddlers don't want to stop playing to get their diapers changed or eat meals. Young children don't want to stop what they're doing to pee or poop. Older kids don't want to come in at night to take a bath. All of this reminds me of a quote by comedian Jerry Seinfeld: *The human body is like a condominium. The thing that keeps you from really enjoying it is the maintenance.*

One of my friends told me that boys wet the bed more often than girls.

Your friend is correct. Boys wet the bed twice as often as girls. Interestingly, girls are more likely than boys to have daytime bladder symptoms such as urgency, frequency, or wetting.

When I was teaching my daughter how to squeeze her sphincter muscle, it reminded me of the Kegel exercises I did after childbirth. Are they related?

When a woman does a Kegel exercise, she's contracting a group of muscles called the *pelvic floor*. The urethra passes through the pelvic floor and the sphincter muscle encircles the urethra. The muscles in the pelvic floor do not contract independently from each other. As a result, when you squeeze the sphincter muscle, you contract the entire pelvic floor, including the muscles around the anus. Therefore, from a "feeling" perspective, contracting one's sphincter muscle is the same as doing a Kegel.

CHAPTER 3

Why Kids Wet the Bed

When I see children for bedwetting visits, one of the questions I ask is why they think they're wet at night. Here are some of the answers I get:

- "Because I'm a deep sleeper."
- "Because I drink too much after dinner."
- "Because I have a small bladder."

Children usually feel bad about wetting the bed, so I let them know right away that bedwetting is not their fault. And as soon as I'm sure that a medical problem isn't causing the wetting (it usually isn't), I tell my patients there's nothing wrong with them, either. In most cases, bedwetting occurs because your brain and your bladder aren't "talking to each other" while you sleep. To understand what this means, I need to explain how we learn to be dry at night and what can keep us from reaching this goal.

Learning to Control Your Bladder

When a baby's bladder fills up with urine, he pees suddenly and doesn't even know it happened. The reason this occurs is because for babies, peeing is a reflex action. (A *reflex action* is something that occurs automatically.) When babies get to be around 18 months old, something interesting takes place. The bladder still works automatically, but now a signal is sent to the brain letting the baby know that he peed. The baby can't control his bladder at this age, but he feels the urine when it comes out.

Most children become potty trained between 2 and 4 years of age. Children learn to use the potty for 2 reasons. First, the bladder gets bigger so it can hold more urine before it fills up. Second, older children develop the ability to hold back urine until they can get to the bathroom. Instead of being a reflex action, peeing is now something kids learn to control. Young children continue to wear diapers at night even though they use the potty during the day. The reason kids need diapers at night is because it takes more time for the brain to figure out what the bladder is doing when you're sleeping than when you're awake.

FUN FACT Has your doctor ever checked your knee reflexes with a little rubber hammer? This usually takes place when you're sitting on the examination table with your legs hanging over the side. The doctor checks your knee reflex by tapping right below your kneecap with the hammer. When the doctor hits the right spot, your leg jumps a bit. Your brain does not control this jumping, although you can see and feel it happen. This reflex action is similar to what happens when a baby pees.

Children usually learn to be dry at night between 3 and 5 years of age. Although some kids get up in the middle of the night to pee, most sleep until morning and go to the bathroom after they wake up. Children learn to be dry at night in 2 steps. First, if the bladder sends a signal to the brain saying that it's filling up with urine, the brain sends a signal back telling the bladder to relax. When the bladder relaxes, it's able to hold more urine and the child sleeps till morning. Second, if the bladder can't hold all of the urine until morning, it wakes the brain up so you can go to the bathroom and pee. Bedwetting occurs because of a delay in learning these 2 skills.

The final step that leads to a wet bed occurs if your brain doesn't "hear" your bladder in the middle of the night. At first your bladder says (in bladder talk), "Timmy, I've got to go, it's time to wake up." Your brain doesn't hear the signal.

A little while later, as your bladder fills up with more urine, it says more loudly, "Timmy, I've got to go, it's time to wake up!" Your brain still doesn't hear the signal.

Finally, as your bladder fills up with even more urine, it screams, "TIMMY, I'VE GOT TO GO, IT'S TIME TO WAKE UP!!!" If your brain misses the signal this time, your bladder can't hold the urine anymore and you wet the bed.

Things That Contribute to Bedwetting

Now that you know how your bladder works, let's discuss some additional facts about bedwetting. Here are the main factors that have an effect on wetting the bed.

Family History

It's well known that bedwetting runs in families. Most children who wet the bed have at least one parent (or another close relative) who had the same problem as a child.

Small Bladder

Having a small bladder is one of the main causes of bedwetting. Small bladders don't hold as much urine as normal-sized bladders. Children with small bladders need to pee more often than their friends and sometimes have to run to the bathroom to avoid having accidents. When you're sleeping at night, a small bladder is less able to relax and hold all of your urine until morning.

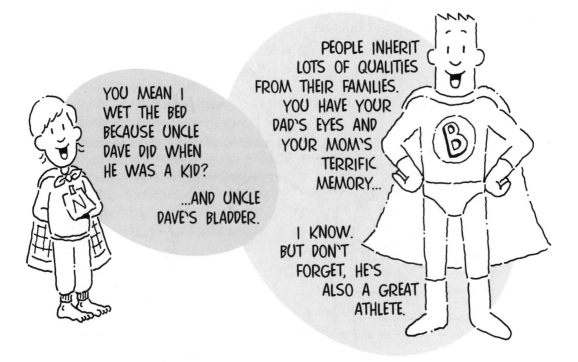

Deep Sleep

Do you remember the experiment in Chapter 2 on page 14 ("Hands On") that explained how the nerves in your bladder send a signal to your brain telling you it's time to pee? Do you remember how you closed your eyes before your coach touched your hand? You knew instantly if it was your left or right hand that was being touched. What do you think would happen if your coach touched your hand while you were sleeping? Do you think you would wake up or continue to sleep? Most children would continue to sleep because their brain wouldn't pay attention to a gentle touch while they were sleeping. However, if someone pinched your hand while you were asleep, there's a better chance that the signal would "get through" and you'd wake up. This is the same thing that's supposed to happen if your bladder can't hold any more urine at night. Unfortunately, many children sleep so soundly that they don't respond to these signals.

Making Too Much Urine at Night

One of the most amazing things about our urinary system is that the brain and kidney seem to know whether it's day or night. Because people sleep at night, it would be silly if our kidneys continued to make the same amount of urine as they do during the day. We'd either need a huge bladder to store it all or we'd have to get up 3 times a night to pee. Our bodies figured out a cool solution to this problem—the brain makes a chemical at night that tells the kidney to make less urine while we sleep. Some children don't produce enough of this chemical and wet the bed because the extra urine overloads their bladders.

Constipation

Constipation is the word we use to describe what happens if people have poops that are hard to pass. If you look at the picture in Chapter 2 on page 9, you'll see that the *rectum* (RECK-tum) is right behind the bladder. (The rectum is the place where poop sits before you go to the bathroom.) If you have a lot of poop in your rectum, it can push against your bladder and may "confuse" the nerve signals that go from your bladder to your brain. This can lead to both daytime accidents and bedwetting. A child may also have wetting problems if he only goes every 3 days or more. These poops are usually pretty big even if they come out easily. *If you're constipated or have infrequent poops, this needs to be corrected before you start the program.* (See "Coach's Corner" on page 24.)

Minor Illness and Fatigue

Illness and fatigue do not cause bedwetting, but they can trigger episodes of wetting by affecting how you sleep at night. In other words, if you're sick or tired, you are less likely to respond to a full bladder when you're sleeping. Although you can't control when you get sick, it's important to go to bed at a reasonable hour so you get a good night's sleep. It also helps if you go to bed no more than an hour later on Friday and Saturday nights.

THE AVERAGE 5- TO 9-YEAR-OLD NEEDS 10 TO 11 HOURS OF SLEEP AT NIGHT, AND THE AVERAGE 10- TO 14-YEAR-OLD NEEDS 9 TO 10 HOURS. BY THE TIME KIDS TURN 18, THEY NEED ABOUT 8 HOURS OF SLEEP.

FUN FACT

Depending on where you live, there are many different ways to say, "I have to go to the bathroom." My favorite expressions are, "I have to go to the can," and "I need to use the powder room." I thought it would be fun to find out how people refer to bathrooms in different settings and other countries. To test your smarts, match the expression in the left-hand column with the place of origin on the right.

1. The washroom	a. Mexico
2. The loo	b. The Navy
3. The necessary	c. Australia
4. The head	d. Canada
5. Les toilettes	e. Germany
6. Los servicios	f. Italy
7. Johnny on the spot	g. England
8. The dunny	h. Colonial America
9. Die Toilette	i. France
10. Il gabinetto	j. Portable toilet

Correct answers: 1 (d), 2 (g), 3 (h), 4 (b), 5 (i), 6 (a), 7 (j), 8 (c), 9 (e), 10 (f)

COACH'S CORNER

My son is dry when he sleeps at his grandmother's house, but he's always wet at home.

It's not uncommon for children to be dry if they sleep at a relative's house. Although this sometimes convinces parents that bedwetting is deliberate, it isn't. When children are dry in this situation, it's because their sleep is somehow altered when they're not in the comfort of their own homes. If you look at this from another perspective, having success away from home is actually reassuring because it shows that your son can be dry at night.

continued on next page

COACH'S CORNER
continued

What do you mean when you say that children wet the bed because they have a small bladder?

This is a good question. When children with small bladders are examined under anesthesia, their bladders are actually normal in size. This means that the bladder is not anatomically small, but the child has the "sensation" that the bladder is full before it really is. The actual medical term for this condition is a small *functional bladder capacity*. I chose the simpler term for kids because it's easier to understand.

My son has a bowel movement every 3 days. I don't understand how this affects his being dry at night.

Infrequent stools (or constipation) can affect bedwetting in 2 ways. First, as mentioned under "Constipation" on pages 21 and 22, a full rectum can "confuse" the nerve signals that are sent to the brain. Second, a full rectum may reduce how much urine the bladder can hold or how well the bladder empties when a child pees. This may sound complicated, but one thing is clear—if a child has a bedwetting problem, his bladder will function better if he has a soft or well-formed stool every day.

There are 2 ways to help children have regular stools—diet and medication. The first thing to do is to adjust the diet according to the Table. In many cases, you can achieve success by cutting back on constipating foods rather than asking children to eat foods they don't like. If this doesn't work, talk to your doctor or nurse practitioner about adding a stool softener to your child's diet. If your child has a more serious problem such as stool withholding or soiling, you should not do the program without medical supervision (see Appendix B).

Foods That Make Stools Harder	Foods That Make Stools Softer
• Milk, cheese, and yogurt	• Fruits and vegetables
• White rice, white breads, and crackers	• Whole grain breads and cereals
• Apples and bananas	• Water and juice (apple is okay)

One of my friends told me that her daughter's bedwetting resolved when she took milk out of her diet.

Although some doctors recommend elimination diets for children who wet at night, there is little research to support this approach. Because many children are picky eaters to begin with, I have not made diet therapy a regular part of my program. There are some foods and beverages that can make a child produce more urine, however, so it's a good idea to avoid these things at dinner. These include chocolate, salty foods, and drinks that contain caffeine (eg, cola, some brands of root beer, tea, coffee).

Having said this, it's not unreasonable to try an elimination diet if you suspect a food sensitivity and it's not a big imposition on your child. The foods that have been implicated with bedwetting most often include milk and milk products, citrus fruits, drinks with citric acid, chocolate, wheat, and corn. If you decide to explore this option, remove these foods from your child's diet for 2 weeks. If you don't see a change in her wetting pattern, dietary factors are not causing the problem. If you do see a change, the next step is to identify which food (or foods) is the culprit. Reintroduce one food to your child's diet every 7 days (the food should be eaten daily during this period). If the wetting recurs, eliminate the food, wait until she's dry again, and proceed to the next food on your list. After a few weeks, you should be able to determine which food(s) is causing the wetting. (If you take milk products out of your child's diet, talk to your doctor or nurse practitioner about providing other sources of calcium and vitamin D.)

My 9-year-old snores at night and one of my friends told me this could cause bedwetting.

There are different ways that children snore. Most of the time, they're just noisy at night, but their breathing is steady and comfortable. Some children have a problem called *obstructive sleep apnea*. Children with this condition not only snore, they have difficulty breathing and make intermittent gasping sounds as they try to get air into their lungs. The problem is usually caused by large adenoids or tonsils. The connection between obstructive apnea and bedwetting is unclear, although we hear stories of children whose bedwetting resolves after they've had surgery to correct their breathing. What's most important here is the apnea, not the bedwetting. If your child has significant snoring at night,

continued on next page

COACH'S CORNER

continued

you should discuss this with your doctor or nurse practitioner.

Why does my daughter wet some nights and not others?

I know it seems odd that children can be wet 3 nights in a row, dry for 5 nights, and then wet again the following night. No one knows why this happens, but it probably has to do with fluctuations in those factors that make them wet in the first place—how much urine they produce during the night, the ability of their bladders to hold urine, and how easily they arouse from sleep.

My 8-year-old son has attention-deficit/hyperactivity disorder (ADHD). One of my friends told me that this would make it harder for him to become dry at night.

Although ADHD does not cause bedwetting, children with attention issues are more likely to wet the bed than other kids. The reason for this association is not clear, but it probably has something to do with the subtle neurologic differences that underlie both conditions. Some authors report that 40% of children with ADHD wet the bed, though this number seems inflated based on my experience.

Over the years, I have successfully treated many children with ADHD and bedwetting. Although it's a little more difficult to help these kids, the problems you run into are just what you'd expect—lack of focus, inattention, and impulse control problems that make it harder for them to stay on task. In addition, some children with ADHD also have learning problems, which can make it harder for them to understand the nuances of the program. Therefore, when I see children with ADHD (or learning disabilities), I make the program as straightforward as possible (see "Coach's Corner" on page 133).

If your child takes medicine for his ADHD, it will help if he's on one of the newer medications that lasts into the early evening. Alternatively, you could give him a small dose of a quick-acting preparation around 4:00 pm to help him stay focused. If your child gets frustrated with the program, keep in mind that children with ADHD may already be suffering from self-esteem issues at school, and wetting the bed only adds to their embarrassment. Finally, it will improve your child's odds of becoming dry if you use the book with medical support instead of doing it on your own.

My husband stopped in our 9-year-old's room the other night before he went to sleep. As he peeked in the door at 11:00 pm, Billy said, "Hi, Dad," and then urinated in his bed. My husband is convinced our son is too lazy to get out of bed at night.

Although I can understand how your husband would arrive at this conclusion, he's wrong. Billy probably has what we refer to as an arousal disorder. What this means is that Billy is unaware of the physical signals his body produces at night. Children like Billy are often described as "deep sleepers," but what's really going on is they can't rouse from one sleep state to another.

When Billy said hello to his dad he was not really awake and had no idea that he peed in the bed. Some children think they're in the bathroom when they wet at night. It seems their bladder has roused them just enough to have a vague sense that they need to urinate, but they're not awake enough to know where they are so they "dream" they're in the bathroom. It's not until they wet the bed that some of them wake up and realize what happened. Other kids don't even wake up when they urinate, or they wake up later in the night (long after the wetting episode) when they're in a lighter state of sleep. The most important thing in this circumstance is that no one makes Billy feel bad for his wetting. The bedwetting alarm and Waking Up Practice are the 2 aspects of the program that address this issue. That's where you should put your energy.

Do psychological problems cause bedwetting?

Although children may develop secondary bedwetting after an episode of emotional stress, psychological problems do not cause primary bedwetting (see Chapter 4 for definitions). Examples of stressful situations that can trigger nighttime wetting include moving to a new home, changing schools, or the death of a loved one. The wetting usually resolves when the stress passes. Keep in mind, however, that bedwetting itself is very stressful for some children and, as a result, can be the cause of anger, social withdrawal, or poor self-esteem.

continued on next page

COACH'S CORNER
continued

My sister-in-law says that punishing a child is the best way to stop bedwetting.

Punishing a child for wetting the bed is not something that health care professionals would ever suggest, even though caregivers may resort to this approach out of frustration and anger. Punishment comes in many forms—a child could be grounded for wetting the bed; she could be sent to her room without dessert; or she might be spanked. *Punishment does not work!* If you have punished your child in the past, tell her why you thought it would help. After you have this discussion, a simple apology is in order, not only to make your child feel better, but because it "cleans the slate" before you begin the program.

We're all human, so it's not unreasonable to get frustrated or angry when children are wetting at night or not cooperating with the program. If you find yourself ready to "blow," take a deep breath and think of another way to vent your emotions. Talk to your spouse, a friend, or a medical professional. If you spend a little time taking care of yourself, you will have more energy to help your child attain her dream of becoming dry at night.

My 8-year-old started wetting the bed 3 weeks after she began taking Zoloft.

Medication occasionally triggers secondary bedwetting. Drugs that have been known to cause this problem include antidepressants like sertraline hydrochloride (Zoloft), antihistamines, and others. In some cases, changing the time that you give the medication or adjusting the dose may control the wetting. Never make an adjustment in any prescription medication without first consulting your doctor, however.

Is there a medication for children who make too much urine at night?

The chemical that reduces urine production at night is called vasopressin. There is a synthetic form of this chemical that helps some children control their bedwetting. I discuss this in more detail in Chapter 27.

Do urinary tract infections cause bedwetting?

Most children who wet the bed have done so for years, and bladder infections are rarely the cause of the problem. If your child suddenly started bedwetting, a bladder infection may be the cause. Bladder infections are easily discovered when the doctor or nurse practitioner examines your child's urine in the office.

CHAPTER 4

What Type of Wetting Do You Have?

Now that we've reviewed how your body works and why kids wet at night, let's figure out what type of bedwetting you have. The best way to do this is to ask you some questions about your bladder habits. Before we get to the questions, however, I want to teach you some of the words we use to describe different types of wetting.

- **Nighttime wetting.** This describes children who wet the bed when they're sleeping. Although most children do this at night, it also applies to children who wet the bed when they're napping.

- **Daytime wetting.** This describes children who wet themselves when they're awake.

- **Primary wetting.** This describes children who never learned to be dry at night. They may have had brief periods of dryness, but they were never dry for more than 6 months in a row.

- **Secondary wetting.** This describes children who were dry for 6 months or more, but then began wetting again.

Mini-Questionnaire

Before you answer the following questions, I should mention that you can combine bedwetting words in lots of ways. For example, you can have nighttime wetting, daytime wetting, or both. You can have primary nighttime wetting or secondary daytime wetting, and so forth. Although this may seem confusing, the type of wetting you have affects how doctors treat you. (Ask your coaches for help if it's too hard to answer question #4.)

1. Do you wet the bed when you're sleeping? ☐ Yes ☐ No

2. Have you ever been dry at night for
   6 months in a row or more? ☐ Yes ☐ No

3. Do you wet your underpants during the day? ☐ Yes ☐ No
   (If you have damp underpants once or twice a week
   because you wait too long to go to the bathroom, you
   should answer "no." If your underpants are damp more
   often or they are actually wet during the day, you should
   answer "yes.")

4. The type of wetting I have is _____.

Most of the children I see for bedwetting visits have *primary
nighttime wetting.* If you have daytime wetting or you started
wetting after being dry for 6 months, you should not use the book
without your doctor's or nurse practitioner's help.

KID'S ALERT

Before you start the program, your coaches need to pay attention to what you do in the bathroom for a couple of days. Please cooperate with them even if it grosses you out a little. The information they collect is very important for the program.

COACH'S CORNER

Why do I need to fill out a questionnaire about my son's bowel and bladder habits?

At the end of the introduction, I mentioned that the book is not intended for children with complicated forms of bedwetting. I did not explain what I meant by this statement at the time, but I'd like to now. Complicated forms of bedwetting have another component that makes them more difficult to treat. Here are some examples:

- A child with daytime and nighttime wetting
- A child with stool soiling and nighttime wetting
- A child with a medical or psychological problem that's causing or directly affecting bedwetting (eg, diabetes, sickle cell disease, certain developmental or psychiatric disorders)

In each of these cases, bedwetting is either secondary to or complicated by another problem, and that problem needs to be addressed before the bedwetting can be treated. Although the program can still work in these situations, you should get professional help before proceeding. In other words, if you plan to use the book on your own, your child's diagnosis should be primary nighttime wetting. Fortunately, this applies to 85% of children who wet the bed. The Health Screening Questionnaire in Appendix B is designed to uncover medical conditions that your doctor or nurse practitioner should be aware of.

Is it difficult to fill out the Health Screening Questionnaire?

When kids are little, parents have a pretty good sense of their elimination patterns. Once children reach the age of 5 or 6 years, most parents fall out of the "poop loop" and are less knowledgeable about what goes on in the bathroom. Before you answer the questions, you must spend a few days observing your child's bowel and bladder habits. Read the questionnaire before you start and keep a record of your observations so you can answer the questions accurately. (A good time to do this is when your child is determining the size of his bladder—see Chapter 8). Be aware that you can't take your child's word for what's happening in the bathroom because kids will often tell you what they think you want to hear. For example, constipated children sometimes "go" everyday, but they produce small, hard stools instead of larger ones that are soft or normally formed.

continued on next page

COACH'S CORNER
continued

Is there another term that doctors use for bedwetting?

Nocturnal enuresis (en-you-REE-sis) is the medical term for bedwetting, and *diurnal* (die-UR-nal) *enuresis* is the medical term for daytime wetting. I substituted the word "wetting" for enuresis in the chapter because it's an easier term for kids to use.

My child only wets the bed twice a week. Is he a good candidate for your program?

This is an interesting question. Someone who wets the bed twice a week is probably a year or so away from becoming dry on his own. In addition, I have found that the bedwetting alarm is less successful with these children because they don't wet often enough to learn what the alarm is designed to teach. If your child is motivated to become dry and does all 4 steps of his Dry-Bed Homework (see Chapter 6), there is a way to increase the efficacy of the alarm—give him a glass of water right before he goes to sleep. This increases the chances that he will wet the bed and, paradoxically, will also improve the usefulness of the alarm.

CHAPTER 5

Pop Quiz

Okay, kids, it's time to take a break from all the hard work you've been doing. The following quiz reviews some of the basic facts about your body and how you become dry at night. I'm not keeping score, though, so it's not like the tests you take at school. (Circle the correct answers.)

1. Why does your body make urine?

   a. Because it gives you a reason to leave your classroom during the day

   b. So toilets would be invented

   c. Because you need a way to get waste products out of your body

2. What organ in your body makes urine?

   a. Your brain

   b. Your liver

   c. Your kidneys

3. Where are your kidneys located?

   a. In your chest

   b. In your bottom

   c. Behind your intestines

4. Where is urine stored before you go to the bathroom?

   a. In your stomach

   b. In your feet

   c. In your bladder

5. What is your bladder made of?

   a. Skin

   b. Silly Putty

   c. Muscle

6. How many children wet the bed in the United States?

   a. 10,000

   b. 50,000

   c. 5 million

7. Why do children wet the bed?

   a. Because they don't eat their vegetables

   b. Because they watch too much TV

   c. Because they are deep sleepers and/or have small bladders

8. How do you know when it's time to pee during the day?

   a. Your mom reminds you

   b. You can't stand up anymore because you're trying so hard not to pee in your pants

   c. You get a tickle or pressure feeling in your bladder

9. Which of the following can contribute to bedwetting?

   a. Eating too much junk food

   b. Forgetting to walk the dog

   c. Constipation

10. Who does most of the work in the Waking Up Dry Program?

   a. Your doctor

   b. Your coach

   c. You

11. Why do some kids run to the bathroom at the last minute when they have to pee?

    a. Because they're having so much fun doing their homework

    b. To drive their parents crazy

    c. Because they ignore their bladder signals until the last second

12. Which of the following is *not* a reflex action?

    a. Babies peeing in their diaper

    b. Yelling at little brothers if they pester you

    c. Older kids peeing in the bathroom

13. What's the name of the muscle you squeeze to hold in your urine?

    a. Your biceps

    b. Your gluteus maximus

    c. Your sphincter muscle

14. Does bedwetting run in families?

    a. No

    b. Maybe

    c. Yes

15. What part of your body is responsible for sending bladder signals to your brain?

    a. Your bones

    b. Your tonsils

    c. Your nerves

16. Why do doctors check your urine at bedwetting visits?

    a. To figure out how tall you'll be when you grow up

    b. To see if you're drinking enough milk

    c. To make sure your kidneys and bladder are healthy

17. How is the bladder like a balloon?

    a. They both come in lots of cool colors

    b. They both pop if you fill them up and toss them out a window

    c. They both stretch when they fill up with liquid

18. What is the most successful treatment for bedwetting?

    a. Eating tree bark

    b. Staying up late at night

    c. The bedwetting alarm

Answer Key: The correct answer for each question is c.

PART 2

Are You Ready to Become Dry?

CHAPTER 6

Dry-Bed Homework

When I see children for their yearly checkups, I ask them lots of questions. I ask about school. I ask about the foods they eat. I ask if they have any questions about their health. I also ask if they are dry at night. If I find out that someone wets the bed, I ask her if she'd like to be dry. This may sound like a silly question, but lots of 4- to 6-year-olds don't mind being wet at night. This is especially true if they wear Pull-Ups to bed. When kids get to be 7 or 8, they almost always want to be dry. There is a big difference, however, between someone who *wants* to be dry and someone who is *ready* to be dry. If a child says she wants to be dry, she may only mean that she wishes her bedwetting went away. This is similar to wishing that you'll get a certain present for your birthday—it's something you want, but you don't have to do anything special to get it. A child isn't ready to be dry until she is willing to do the work it takes to reach that goal. In this chapter, I'm going to help you find out how ready you are to become dry.

Teaching children about the Waking Up Dry Program requires 2 visits to my office. At the first visit, I find out how often they pee and poop, and I ask about their nighttime wetting. After I talk with them for a while, I do a checkup and have them pee in a cup so I can examine their urine. Once I make sure that a medical problem isn't causing their bedwetting, I teach them how their body makes urine and why kids wet the bed at night. At the end of the visit, I give kids a job to do called their Dry-Bed Homework. This home-work assignment has 2 goals. First, it gets me some additional information I need for the program. Second, it lets me know how motivated they are to become dry. If a child is interested in the things we discussed and does her homework, then I know she's ready to work on the program.

Dry-Bed Homework

Before you start your homework, stop any measures you've been doing to control your bedwetting, including Pull-Ups. That way, you'll get a good picture of your wetting pattern before you start the program. You need to do your homework for *2 weeks* before you "score" it. The reason for this is that while some steps are only performed once, others need to be done every day. And the best way to test your motivation is to find out if you can stick with something for more than a few days. I'll show you how to score your homework in Chapter 11.

Here is the assignment that I want you to do. It's the same one I give to my patients after our first visit.

1. Start paying attention to your bladder. This means you should go to the bathroom as soon as you feel the urge to pee. Also, you should cooperate with your coaches if they ask you to pee before bed or before you leave the house even if you *don't* feel the need to go.

2. Make a Waking Up Dry Calendar and record whether you are wet or dry when you get up in the morning (see Chapter 7).

3. Find out the size of your bladder (see Chapter 8).

4. Do the Alarm Clock Test (see Chapter 9).

KID'S ALERT

Continue to read the book while you're doing the Dry-Bed Homework. That way you'll be ready to start the program as soon as you score your homework.

Sometimes kids prefer to do a few simple things to control their bedwetting instead of doing the regular program. In this situation, we set up an easy version like the one described in "Katie's Story."

Katie's Story

Katie is a 6-year-old girl who saw me for a checkup a few months ago. During the visit, I found out that Katie wet the bed every night. I knew Katie's wetting was not caused by a medical problem because she was a healthy girl who had no problems with peeing or pooping in the daytime. Katie did not want to wear Pull-Ups anymore, but she got upset if she woke up in a wet bed.

When I described the Waking Up Dry Program, Katie said that she preferred doing some easy things to control her bedwetting. This meant that she skipped the Dry-Bed Homework and the bed-wetting alarm. I agreed with Katie's decision, and this is the program we set up.

- Katie made a calendar to keep track of her dry nights. Katie decided to call it her *Dry-Bed Calendar.* She also decided that she would put stickers on the calendar whenever she had a dry night.
- Katie's mom encouraged her to drink an extra glass of water during the day. Katie liked this idea because her mom said she could have crackers or pretzels with the water.

continued on next page

Katie's Story, continued

- Katie agreed to go to the bathroom whenever she felt the urge to pee.
- Every night before she went to sleep, Katie got in bed and her mom reminded her about the tickle feeling that told her it was time to pee. As she lay in bed, she imagined that her bladder was filling up like a balloon fills up with water. When she imagined that her bladder was as big as an orange, Katie got up and went to the bathroom to pee. As her mom snuggled her in bed, they said the following message together: "If I need to pee at night, I will wake up all by myself and go to the bathroom."
- Katie's mom put special pads on the bed to make cleanup easier in the morning.
- Some days, Katie didn't feel like doing the program. When this happened, her mom did not push the issue.
- Katie's parents gave her a few small rewards for cooperating with the program—an extra book before bed, some extra TV time on the weekend, or a special outing with her mom or dad.

Katie did not become dry right away, but she liked being in charge of her body. After doing her program for a few months, she was dry 3 to 4 nights a week. Katie was very proud of her accomplishment.

COACH'S CORNER

Is it necessary to do the Dry-Bed Homework?

The mainstay of my program is the bed-wetting alarm, and my goal is to encourage all children 7 years and older to use this device. (I occasionally see 6-year-olds who are motivated enough the use the alarm). I have learned through experience, however, that many children are not ready to be woken up night after night. I developed the Dry-Bed Homework because it identifies children who are more likely to drop out of the program when the reality of the alarm hits. I think it's better to take a more modest approach with these youngsters than to have them deal with disappointment days or weeks into using the alarm. Articles in medical journals report that up to 25% of children drop out of treatment. My dropout rate is less than 10% because I screen kids before we start.

Can you gauge a child's motivation by the way he approaches his Dry-Bed Homework?

This is a good question. It's important to realize that each child is different. Some children like to talk about becoming dry, and others don't. Some kids ask lots of questions about the program, and others don't. Some kids are hesitant when they try something new, while others dive right in. Some kids are perfectionists and get easily frustrated if things don't work well right away. Some children are more embarrassed about the problem than others, and these kids are usually less interested in talking about their wetting. Also, if parents have punished or reprimanded the child in the past, he may be ambivalent about starting something new. This is equally true for kids who have tried other methods in the past and did not become dry.

You know your child better than anyone, so take that knowledge and apply it to the way he approaches the Dry-Bed Homework. As always, remember to be honest with your child. At the start of the homework, let him know in an upbeat manner that the way he does these tasks will determine how you proceed with the program. If your child is outwardly enthusiastic and does all of the work, it's easy. If your child is less vocal but still does all of the work, he is probably just as motivated. If you sense some hesitation on your child's part or recognize personality traits that might make things more difficult, be

continued on next page

COACH'S CORNER
continued

encouraging and see if you can motivate him to do the work. Remind him of past accomplishments and how he succeeded if he stuck with something. You can also say things like, "Jason, it's normal to be unsure of yourself when you're starting something new. But I know you can do it!"

My sister-in-law told me that her daughter became dry after one visit to the doctor.

Every few months, I see a child who becomes dry right after our first visit or during the 2 weeks that she is doing the Dry-Bed Homework. I'm not sure why this happens, though I suspect the child was close to being dry on her own and paying attention to the problem nudged her over the fence. Everyone is delighted when this occurs, though I warn parents that the effect may be temporary. If this happens to you, praise your child for her success, but be prepared for a relapse once the "honeymoon period" is over. If she starts wetting again, stay relaxed and pick up where you left off. Let her read this paragraph so she knows this happens to other kids and that it's nothing to worry about. On the other hand, if your child stays dry for 2 weeks, a relapse is unlikely.

My 6-year-old wets the bed 3 times a week. He's not interested in working on becoming dry, but he hides his wet underpants in his closet.

Most children are embarrassed about wetting the bed, and the younger ones will often resort to hiding their wet clothes as a means to avoid the problem. Have a nonthreatening discussion with your son about what he's doing. Let him know that you understand why he's hiding his underwear, but that it's unsanitary to leave wet clothes around the house. If possible, share a secret from your own childhood to help him see that you understand what he's going through. In addition, consider giving him some rewards for being more responsible with his wet clothes. This doesn't have to be anything elaborate. Set up a progress chart and give him a sticker every time he puts his underpants in the laundry basket. When he gets 5 stickers on his chart, let him choose a restaurant for dinner or get some extra TV time. Encourage him to make the chart himself, and make sure you purchase the stickers together.

CHAPTER 7

Waking Up Dry Calendar

When children learn to overcome their bedwetting, they do not become dry right away. Like any other skill, they get better with time. Some children become dry in a few weeks; others take a few months. To follow your progress, it's important to keep a record of wet and dry nights.

Keeping a calendar does 2 things. First, it lets you know when you reach your goal of being dry 14 nights in a row. Second, because it's easy to get discouraged while you're waiting to become dry, the calendar lets you follow the progress you make along the way. For example, let's say you wet the bed every night before you start the program. Then, by the time you're 4 weeks into it, you're wet every other night. You might be disappointed because you've been doing the program for a long time and you're still wetting the bed. By looking at the calendar, however, you'd see that your wetting has decreased from 7 nights a week to 3. This is terrific progress, but you wouldn't know it if you didn't keep a calendar.

KID'S ALERT The first 2 weeks that you use the calendar is part of your Dry-Bed Homework. Once you begin the program, you will continue to use the calendar to follow your progress.

Setting Up Your Calendar

1. Make or buy a calendar that looks like the one on page 51. This is the best type of calendar to use because you can see a month at a time, which makes it easier to follow your progress. If you decide to buy a calendar, go shopping with your coach so you can pick it out.

2. Notice that the example on page 51 shows 3 different ways to mark your calendar. If you have a completely dry night, write *D* for *dry.* If your underpants are wet but the sheet and blanket are dry, write *SW* for *small wet.* If you wet your sheets or blanket in addition to your underpants, write *LW* for *large wet.*

3. I recommend keeping track of large and small wet spots because children usually become dry in stages—they start out with large spots and then have smaller ones, until they finally become dry. By keeping a record of both sizes, it's easier to follow your progress. This is especially helpful at the beginning of the program, when it's important to see even small improvements in your wetting.

4. Some kids prefer using stickers or stars when they have dry nights instead of writing *D* on their calendar. If you choose this method, make sure the stickers are small enough to fit inside the space.

5. If you wet more than once a night, you should mark each episode on your calendar.

6. Once you begin the program, it also helps to keep track of your nighttime waking habits. If you wake up on your own when the bedwetting alarm goes off, put a check mark (✓) on your calendar.

7. Keep the calendar in your bedroom because you'll need to fill it in every morning after you wake up. If you forget to mark the calendar, your coaches will remind you to do it.

8. Most children put their calendars in a drawer or closet as soon as they record what happened during the night. If you leave it lying around, you may forget to put it away later. This could be embarrassing if a friend comes over after school and sees the calendar.

KID'S ALERT

Some children are very disappointed when they have a wet night. This is especially true if they've been dry for a number of days before they're wet. If this happens to you, you might be tempted to argue with your coaches that the bed was dry. It's important to know that your sheets and underpants may *look* dry in the morning, even though they were wet the night before. Adults are better than kids at seeing urine stains or noticing the smell of urine in your room. Please remember that your coaches want you to be dry as much as you do. If they say you had a wet night, you should believe them.

9. In the morning, you and your coaches should review whether you were wet or dry during the night.

10. Continue to use your calendar every day that you're doing the Waking Up Dry Program.

KNOCK, KNOCK!

WHO'S THERE?

IRA.

IRA WHO?

IRA MEMBERED TO FILL OUT MY CALENDAR!

COACH'S CORNER

My 9-year-old daughter appears motivated to work on the program, but she forgets to fill out her calendar.

Children aren't as organized as adults, so this isn't unusual and should not be interpreted as a sign of poor motivation. Ask your daughter if she can think of a way to trigger her memory such as putting a note on her bathroom mirror or closet door. If she still forgets, remind her to fill out the calendar before she goes to breakfast. Remember that your tone should be encouraging so she doesn't misinterpret your support as nagging.

My son is a little careless at times. What should we do if someone finds his calendar?

This doesn't happen very often, but it's a good idea to have a response handy in case it does (see Chapter 24).

July

Sunday	Monday	Tuesday	Wednesday	Thursday	Friday	Saturday
				1 LW	2 LW	3 LW
4 SW ✓	5 LW	6 LW	7 LW ✓	8 SW ✓	9 LW	10 SW ✓
11 SW ✓	12 D	13 SW ✓	14 LW	15 D	16 SW ✓	17 D
18 D	19 SW ✓	20 D	21 D	22 D	23 SW ✓	24 SW ✓
25 D	26 SW ✓	27 D	28 D	29 D	30 D	31 D

CHAPTER 8

How Big Is
Your Bladder?

By now you know that your bladder is the place where your body
stores urine until it's time to pee. I mentioned earlier that some
children run to the bathroom at the last minute. Most of the time
this happens because kids are too busy watching TV or playing a
game to stop what they're doing and go to the bathroom. Some
kids have small bladders, however, and they have to pee more
often than their friends. The purpose of this chapter is to find
out the size of your bladder.

The best way to measure your bladder is to keep a 2-day record
of how much you pee each time you go to the bathroom. Although
you don't have to stay home the entire time, it helps to do the
bladder test on a weekend when you don't have many activities
scheduled. Another option is to do it on 2 Saturdays or Sundays so
you don't have to spend an entire weekend focused on your bladder.

Supplies You'll Need at Home

- A 16-ounce plastic measuring cup
- An index card
- A pen or pencil

IT HELPS IF YOU
DRINK AN EXTRA
GLASS OF WATER
EACH DAY THAT YOU
DO THE BLADDER TEST.

How to Measure Your Bladder

1. Keep a pen or pencil, an index card, and a plastic measuring cup in whichever bathroom you usually use at home.

2. When you feel the urge to pee, go to the bathroom and pee in the cup. Boys usually pee standing up. For girls, it may be easier if you sit on the toilet backwards. This pushes your knees apart and gives you more room to place the cup between your legs. (Your coach can hold the cup if you think it will help.)

3. Record how much urine is in the cup (in ounces) on the index card.

4. Empty the cup in the toilet and rinse it out.

5. You don't need to record anything if you pee when you're away from home; however, if you're able to hold back your urine, wait until you get home before going to the bathroom.

6. To get an accurate picture of your bladder size, you should have 8 to 10 measurements. If you don't get this many measurements in 2 days, keep the record for an additional day.

Kids sometimes forget to pee in the measuring cup when they're doing the bladder test. You can prevent this from happening by keeping the toilet seat down or by putting a reminder note on the wall behind the toilet. Can you think of some other tricks that will help you remember to pee in the cup?

- _____

- _____

- _____

- _____

- _____

- _____

TIPS & TRICKS

Whenever you go to the bathroom, it's important to empty your bladder completely. Here are some tips to help you accomplish this:

- If you have to go to the bathroom when you're playing a game or watching TV, don't "pee and run." This means you shouldn't rush to get back to what you were doing. Relax and give your bladder a chance to let out all of your urine.
- For boys: When you go to the bathroom, pull your underpants all the way down. If you bend your penis over the top of your underpants, it makes it harder for all of your urine to come out.
- For girls: When you go to the bathroom, sit back on the toilet seat and separate your legs. If you keep your legs together or sit at the front of the seat, it makes it harder for all of your urine to come out.

Bladder Measurements (in ounces)

Day 1	Day 2	Day 3 (if needed)
_____	_____	_____
_____	_____	_____
_____	_____	_____
_____	_____	_____
_____	_____	_____
_____	_____	_____
_____	_____	_____
_____	_____	_____

How to Tell if Your Bladder Is Small

A child's normal bladder size (in ounces) equals the child's age plus 2. Therefore, the average 6-year-old has a bladder size that is 8 ounces (6 + 2 = 8), while the average 10-year-old has a bladder size that is 12 ounces (10 + 2 = 12). Children who are 12 years and older have a bladder that's the same size as an adult—12 to 16 ounces. If your bladder measures within 2 ounces of these numbers, it's still considered to be "normal." However, if your bladder is more than 2 ounces below these numbers, you have a small bladder (see Table).

My largest bladder measurement is _____.

Bladder Size According to Age

Age	Normal Range (ounces)	Small Bladder (ounces)
6 years	6–10	5 or less
7 years	7–11	6 or less
8 years	8–12	7 or less
9 years	9–13	8 or less
10 years	10–14	9 or less
11 years	11–15	10 or less
12 years and older	12–16	11 or less

FUN FACT Have you ever wondered how much urine animals make? Because mammals have bladders, they pee just like people do. Well, not just like people, because they pee on the ground instead of in a toilet. Here's a list of some popular mammals and the amount of urine they make each day. For comparison purposes, the average human makes about 4 cups (¼ gallon) per day.

- Elephant   208 cups (13 gallons)
- Cow   72 cups (4½ gallons)
- Horse   24 cups (1½ gallons)
- Pig   12 cups (¾ gallon)
- Sheep   8 cups (½ gallon)

If you compare these numbers, you'll find that an elephant produces as much urine in one day as 3 cows, 9 horses, 18 pigs, 26 sheep, or 52 humans. That's a lot of pee!

COACH'S CORNER *Is there any reason to know my son's bladder size, other than finding out if he's willing to cooperate with the program?*

In the past, doctors taught children with small bladders to do "stretching" exercises to try and make their bladders bigger. This treatment has fallen out of favor because it's hard for children to hold back their urine and current research doesn't support this approach. That said, there are 3 reasons why it's worth knowing if a child has a small bladder.

- It's more important for these children to drink water during the day.
- Children with small bladders are less likely to respond to the medication desmopressin (see Chapter 27).
- Children with small bladders sometimes wet the bed more than once a night. If this happens, they may need to add a medication like oxybutynin to the program (see "Wetting the Bed More Than Once Per Night" on page 141 in Chapter 22).

continued on next page

COACH'S CORNER

continued

My son has a small bladder, but his teacher doesn't like it if students leave class day after day to use the bathroom.

As every parent knows, there's no shortage of rules at school. Despite all the regulations, you do have one trump card to play—a note from your doctor or nurse practitioner. I have some patients with small bladders that need to visit the bathroom as soon as their bladder tells them it's time to go. I have other patients with daytime wetting that need to urinate every 2 hours (they wear a special vibrating wristwatch that discretely reminds them to go). As long as I write a note describing their medical need, schools cooperate with my request.

Your focus seems to be on children with small bladders. My daughter has a large bladder, but she still wets the bed.

Because a large bladder capacity is atypical for children with nighttime wetting, your daughter should be examined for constipation or other problems that interfere with normal bladder emptying.

If her evaluation is normal, there are a few strategies that you can incorporate into the program. First, it's important that she urinates regularly during the day. She should go to the bathroom every 2 hours even if she doesn't feel the need to pee. The reason for this is because children with large bladders don't appreciate bladder fullness the way most people do. In addition, regular bathroom habits may "retrain" her bladder over time and allow it to function more normally. I would also suggest that she urinates twice before she goes to sleep—have her go 30 minutes before she gets into bed and then again right before she turns off the light. Finally, it's important that she follows the tip in "Tips & Tricks" on page 55 and remains in the bathroom for a few minutes to give her bladder time to empty.

CHAPTER 9

Alarm Clock Test

The bedwetting alarm is the most effective treatment for learning to be dry at night. However, as I mentioned in the introduction, it also takes the most work. Because lots of kids are deep sleepers, we need to find out if you will wake up when the alarm goes off. The Alarm Clock Test is designed to answer that question.

It takes 3 nights to do the test. On the first night, set the alarm to go off 1 hour after you go to sleep. On the second night, set the alarm to go off 2 hours after you go to sleep. On the third night, set the alarm to go off 3 hours after you go to sleep. You pass the test if you wake up on your own *or* with your coach's help on any of the 3 nights. If you're unable to wake up or you are too sleepy to follow the steps listed below, you're not ready to use the bedwetting alarm.

It's common for children not to wake up on their own when they begin using the bedwetting alarm, and the same thing may occur during the Alarm Clock Test. So don't be discouraged if you're too sleepy at first—that's why the test runs for 3 nights. Also, don't do the test after a really hectic day because it will be harder for you to wake up that night.

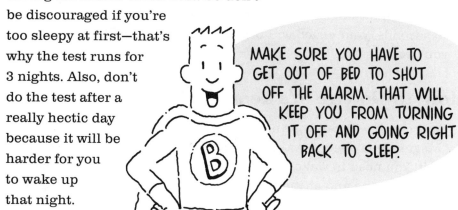

MAKE SURE YOU HAVE TO GET OUT OF BED TO SHUT OFF THE ALARM. THAT WILL KEEP YOU FROM TURNING IT OFF AND GOING RIGHT BACK TO SLEEP.

Supplies You'll Need at Home

- An electric clock with a buzzing alarm
- A wet washcloth

How to Do the Alarm Clock Test

1. Get ready for bed the way you normally do—change into your pajamas or nighttime underpants, brush your teeth, and put on your night-light.

2. If you have never used an alarm clock before, your coach will show you how it works. Your coach can set the alarm, but *you* need to be the one to turn it off after it starts to buzz.

3. Before you go to sleep, practice turning off the alarm. Lie down in bed and pretend to be asleep. Have your coach "fast-forward" the time so the alarm goes off. Wake up from your pretend sleep and quickly turn off the alarm. Go to the bathroom to pee and return to your room.

4. As you fall asleep, tell yourself that you will pay attention to the alarm and that you will wake up as soon as it goes off. Remind yourself that you are the boss of your body!

5. Your coach should go to your room a few minutes before the alarm is set to go off.

6. If you wake up when the alarm goes off, sit up and quickly turn it off. Go to the bathroom to pee and then go back to sleep.

7. If you don't wake up after the alarm has been buzzing for 10 seconds, your coach will begin the Wake-up Drill to help you get up.

How to Do the Wake-up Drill

1. Your coach will call your name and say the wake-up message. "Maggie, you need to wake up! Wake up, Maggie! Maggie, you can do it! You need to wake up if you want to have dry beds!" (**Coach's Tip:** Your tone and attitude should be animated and encouraging.)

IF YOU HAPPEN TO BE WET WHEN THE ALARM GOES OFF, COMPLETE THE ALARM CLOCK TEST. WHEN YOU FINISH GOING TO THE BATHROOM, PUT ON DRY CLOTHES, CHANGE THE BED, AND GO BACK TO SLEEP.

2. If you don't wake up, your coach will gently shake your shoulders 3 or 4 times and repeat the wake-up message.

3. If you still don't wake up, your coach will sit you up in bed and repeat the wake-up message.

4. If you still don't wake up, your coach will wet your face 2 or 3 times with a washcloth and repeat the wake-up message.

5. If you still don't wake up, your coach will repeat the wake-up message and walk you around the room. (**Coach's Tip:** If you're not strong enough to walk your child around the room, stand her up by the side of the bed. If this is too difficult, skip this step. I don't want anyone to get hurt by falling on the floor.)

6. If you wake up at any point during steps 1 to 5, you should quickly turn off the alarm. Go to the bathroom to pee and then go back to sleep.

7. If you don't wake up or you are unwilling to turn off the alarm and go to the bathroom, your coach will turn it off and let you go back to sleep.

GREAT JOB! YOU WOKE UP 2 OUT OF 3 NIGHTS!

COACH'S CORNER

How hard should I shake my child when I try to wake him up at night?

Not hard. Think of it as rocking him back and forth with a gentle motion. Some parents find that tickling their children is more effective than shaking them.

Is it important for children to be fully awake when they do the Alarm Clock Test?

Children do not need to be fully conscious when they do the Alarm Clock Test. However, they should be awake enough to turn off the alarm and go to the bathroom. If your child is groggy, you can guide her through each task, if necessary. Stay close by to ensure that she gets to and from the bathroom safely.

CHAPTER 10

Family Matters

In Chapter 6, we discussed your readiness to become dry at night. Now we need to look at your family to make sure nothing at home will affect your chances of becoming dry. Here are some things to consider before you begin the program.

Vacation

There are 2 reasons why summer can be a good time to do the program: (1) you can usually sleep later in the morning, and (2) you don't have homework or tests to worry about. Despite these advantages, there is one thing about the summer that can make it harder to work on becoming dry—family vacations. If you're planning to go away in the next 2 months, consider delaying the program until your trip is over.

Moving to a New Home

If you're planning to move in the next month, hold off on starting the program until you're settled in your new home.

Illness

If anyone in the family is scheduled to have an operation or is sick with more than a simple problem, consider delaying the program. Your coaches may be distracted at such times, and they're less likely to be able to give you the attention you need.

Brothers and Sisters

Because most of us have siblings (brothers or sisters), certain events can make it harder for the program to work. Here are some things to keep in mind.

- Is your mom about to have a baby?

- Is your family about to adopt a baby?

- Are there 2 children at home who wet the bed? If the answer to this question is "yes," only 1 person should be treated at a time. Logically, the older child should have the chance to go first.

Arguing at Home

This is a hard one to discuss, but if you get angry very easily or you and your parents are arguing a lot about homework or other issues, this may not be a good time to start the program. Learning to become dry takes a lot of cooperation between you and your coaches, so if you're already fighting with each other, the chances are pretty good that you'll fight about the program, too. It's important to note, however, that a little arguing in families is *normal.* If you do have some issues to iron out, this does not mean you can't work on becoming dry. It just means you shouldn't do the program alone with your parents. Work with your doctor or even consider seeing a psychologist (a talking doctor) to help you and your parents work things out.

Family Stress

It's important for the home environment to be supportive and relatively stress-free for the program to work. Therefore, if your parents are under a lot of pressure, this may not be a good time to do the program. If only one of your parents is under stress and the other one is available to help you, then you can go ahead.

COACH'S CORNER

My daughter is jealous over the attention her brother is getting with the program.

To start with, tell your daughter that you're working on a very important program to help your son overcome his bedwetting. You can then do 1 of 2 things to enlist your daughter's help. The first choice is to reward her for being supportive. Just as your son gets to pick out weekly rewards for his efforts (see Chapter 14), your daughter can get some token rewards for encouraging her brother. This has to be acceptable with your son, however, because children may not want siblings to say anything about their bedwetting. Alternatively, you can set up a program with your daughter in which she can earn her own rewards. For example, she can get rewards for cleaning up the house (not regular chores, something extra) or working on one of her own problems like thumb sucking.

I have a 9-year-old daughter who wets the bed, and she doesn't want her brother to know about the program.

This is a little tricky, as everyone is living under the same roof. You should respect your daughter's wishes, however, and try to come up with some practical solutions. Here are a few things that may help.

- Don't talk about the problem if her brother is nearby.
- Find a safe place to keep the book and her Waking Up Dry Calendar.

continued on next page

COACH'S CORNER

continued

- Make sure her brother is doing something when wet bedding is taken to the laundry room (see "Alice's Story" in Chapter 19 on page 123).
- If your daughter goes to sleep after her brother, do Waking Up Practice (see Chapter 12) once he's in bed. If she goes to sleep before him, shut her door when she does the exercise and use a chair in her room as a "pretend" toilet. This will be easier to accomplish if another parent is in charge of her brother.
- If your daughter uses the bedwetting alarm, it will be hard to keep her brother in the dark, even though most siblings don't wake up when the alarm goes off. Just be as discreet as possible, following the same timing advice suggested for Waking Up Practice.

I have an 8-year-old son who wets the bed, and I recently found out that his 10-year-old brother has been threatening to tell his friends about it.

This is a serious situation. Both parents need to sit down with your older son to work this out. Try to avoid any anger or accusations at the beginning of your talk. Let your son know that you found out what's been happening and ask him to explain his side to you. The bottom line, however, is that this behavior is absolutely unacceptable, and you need to convey this to your son. Be very specific about this, and let him know exactly what the consequences will be if he continues to threaten his brother. One final thought—if there are long-standing relationship issues between your children, you should consider seeing a mental health professional to work on the problem.

I was getting ready to start a bedwetting program with my 10-year-old, but his younger brother is having a lot of trouble at school.

There's no such thing as a stress-free home, and the word *multitasking* must have been invented for parents. The question you should ask yourself is whether you can devote energy to both of your children at this time. The bedwetting program usually takes 2 to 3 months to complete, with a fair dose of sleepiness thrown in. If you think you can work through your younger son's problem more quickly, put the bedwetting program on hold for a while.

My 11-year-old daughter wants to use the bedwetting alarm, but our family situation isn't right for the alarm at the moment. What would you recommend?

If your daughter is motivated to work on her bedwetting, consider an approach she can do independently.

- Have your daughter set her alarm clock to go off an hour before she usually wets the bed. When the alarm goes off, she can get up and go to the bathroom on her own. If she has a history of wetting more than once a night, buy a clock that has 2 alarm settings. Remember to put the clock away from her bed so she has to get up to turn it off.

- If your daughter has trouble waking up at night, she may have more success with a clock that's designed for heavy sleepers. The Wake Assure alarm clock buzzes, flashes a bedside lamp, and vibrates the bed in an effort to accomplish this task. You can buy this clock at www.comforthouse.com.

- Have your daughter do the "modified" program described under "Scoring Your Homework" in Chapter 11 on pages 72 to 73.

- Ask your doctor about using the medication desmopressin (see Chapter 27). If this is ineffective or only provides short-term relief, you can reconsider the bedwetting alarm at some point in the future.

My husband and I are divorced. Does this mean my son can't do the program?

If parents are divorced or separated, the program is obviously more difficult to do. Here are some questions to ask yourself before you begin.

- Can you communicate with your ex-husband?
- Does your son see his father regularly?
- Do you and your ex-husband agree on doing the program?

If you and your ex-husband can communicate with each other, it's okay to proceed. It's important that both of you to follow the program the same way, however. If you disagree about certain aspects of the program, discuss this with your child's doctor or nurse practitioner. Also, make sure your son has his calendar and other materials when he travels from one home to the other.

PART 3

Getting Set for the Program

CHAPTER 11

Scoring Your Dry-Bed Homework

When I work with children in my office, I meet with them 2 weeks after our first visit. At this time, I review their Dry-Bed Homework and we set up the program. Because I won't be meeting with you 2 weeks after you do your homework, you'll need another way to do this. If you're doing the program with your doctor or nurse practitioner, he or she can help you build the program. If you're doing the program at home, your coaches will help.

It's important to be honest when you score your homework and remember that your coaches need to agree with you about how things went. For example, the hardest part is the Alarm Clock Test. Sometimes children are very sleepy when the alarm goes off, and they won't get up even when their coaches do the Wake-up Drill. Then, the following morning, they don't remember what happened and think everything went well. Keep in mind that your coaches want you to be dry as much as you do and adults remember what happens at night better than kids. So if your coaches tell you that step 4 didn't go well, you should believe them.

Scoring Your Homework

If you weren't able to complete the first 3 steps of the Dry-Bed Homework, you're not ready to do the program. There are still a few things you can do to help yourself, however, so consider the following options:

1. Read "Katie's Story" on pages 43 and 44 in Chapter 6. If you like her program, you can do all or part of this yourself.

2. If you're younger than 8 years and you don't want to do anything about your wetting, it's okay if you use Pull-Ups at night. Older children should not use Pull-Ups except in special circumstances (see Chapter 25).

3. Talk to your coaches about having one of them take you to the bathroom right before they go to sleep. This is called *lifting* and is discussed in Chapter 25.

If you completed the first 3 steps of the Dry-Bed Homework but not the fourth, you're not ready to use the bedwetting alarm, but there are a number of things you can do to help yourself become dry (I call this the *modified* program).

1. Fill out your Waking Up Dry Calendar every day, keeping track of wet and dry nights.

2. Do Waking Up Practice every night as described in Chapter 12.

3. Do the bladder exercises described in Chapter 13.

4. If you don't make any progress after a few months, you can redo the Alarm Clock Test to see if you're ready to use the bedwetting alarm.

5. If you're still not ready to use the bedwetting alarm, add lifting to the program or talk to your doctor or nurse practitioner about taking a medication to reduce your nighttime wetting (see Chapter 27).

If you completed all 4 steps of the Dry-Bed Homework, you're ready to do the regular program. The next few chapters describe the bedwetting alarm and some extra things you can do that help kids become dry. I will show you how to set up the program in Chapter 20.

COACH'S CORNER

My son is disappointed because he really wanted to use the bedwetting alarm, but he didn't wake up when we did the Alarm Clock Test.

Although the Alarm Clock Test is a good measure of a child's ability to respond to the bedwetting alarm, you have one more option at this point. Tell your son that his cooperation earned him another shot at the test. This time, do it for 5 nights instead of 3. If he's still unable to awaken, remind him that lots of kids are deep sleepers and that his ability to wake up will improve as he gets older. In the meantime, be enthusiastic about the modified program described at the top of this page.

Remember to praise your son for continuing to show any interest in becoming dry. If he has a run of dry nights, consider giving him a reward like a special dessert, some extra TV or computer time, or allowing him to choose a restaurant for dinner.

continued on next page

COACH'S CORNER

continued

My 8-year-old has been doing the modified program for 2 months. She started out wetting the bed every night and now wets 3 or 4 times a week. We tried the Alarm Clock Test, but she was too sleepy to get up. She's still doing the program but her enthusiasm isn't what it used to be.

Although I can appreciate your daughter's frustration, she's made very good progress, considering that she used to wet the bed every night. I mentioned previously that the bedwetting alarm is the most successful treatment for bedwetting. The cure rate for the modified program isn't as good. These children become dry or reduce their wetting frequency 40% to 50% of the time. (See page 106 in Chapter 16 under "Coach's Corner" for statistics on the bedwetting alarm.)

There are a few ways that you can handle your current situation.

- Continue with the modified program. In time, your daughter may have more dry nights per week. If you take this approach, tell her that she's doing very well and to keep up the good work.

- Add lifting to the program, making sure that your daughter is awake enough to walk to the bathroom on her own after your get her up.

- Talk to your doctor or nurse practitioner about adding a medication to the program.

- Stop the program. If you take this approach, tell your daughter that she's done a great job so far, but sometimes it helps to take a breather for a while. You can restart the modified program in 6 to 12 months or redo the Alarm Clock Test to see if she's ready for the bed-wetting alarm.

CHAPTER 12

Waking Up Practice

Most children become dry at night because their bladders learn to hold all of their urine until morning. Others need to wake up if their bladders get full while they're sleeping. Therefore, one of the things that will help you become dry is to learn to wake up if your bladder signals your brain that it can't hold any more urine. Waking Up Practice is an exercise that helps accomplish this task.

Before you do Waking Up Practice, get ready for bed the way you normally do—change into your pajamas or nighttime underpants and turn on your night-light. If you don't use a night-light, you'll need another source of light so you can see what you're doing in the middle of the night. Here are some other options:

- A lamp with a low-wattage bulb
- A ceiling light with a dimmer switch
- A bathroom or hallway light that provides enough brightness in your room

WHEN YOU PEE AT NIGHT, REMEMBER TO STAY IN THE BATHROOM LONG ENOUGH TO EMPTY YOUR BLADDER COMPLETELY.

How to Do Waking Up Practice

1. Lie in bed, close your eyes, and pretend you're asleep.

2. Imagine that your bladder is the size of a plum.

3. Imagine that your bladder is filling up with urine. As your bladder fills up, it gets bigger like a balloon filling up with water.

4. Imagine that your bladder is now the size of an orange. At this size, it sends a signal to your brain telling you that it's time to pee. Concentrate on this feeling.

5. Imagine the tickle or pressure feeling you get during the day when you need to pee, only now the feeling is stronger. Much stronger.

6. Imagine that your bladder is telling your brain it's time to wake up. You need to wake up so you can go to the bathroom and pee. You need to wake up so you will be dry in the morning.

7. Imagine that you are waking up. Open your eyes and quickly squeeze your sphincter muscle to make sure you stay dry. (See the Bladderman tip on page 15 in Chapter 2 for a reminder of how to do this.)

8. Get out of bed, go to the bathroom, and pretend to pee.

9. Go back to your room and lie down. Feel your sheets and imagine waking up in a nice dry bed. Remind yourself that you are going to wake up if your bladder can't hold all of your urine until morning.

10. Remind yourself that you are the boss of your bladder.

TIPS & TRICKS

Kids have a harder time getting up in the winter months when the floor is cold or if it's cold in the home. Therefore, it's helpful to have a carpet or throw rugs on the floor and for the temperature to be set at a comfortable range.

It takes practice to learn to wake up at night, so I'd like you to do the exercise *2 times* before you go to sleep. On your second trip to the bathroom, instead of pretending to pee, you should actually pee in the toilet and then go back to bed.

Your coach should read the 10 steps to you every night for the first week that you're doing the program. (This lets you concentrate on the feelings I describe in the exercise.) After the first week, you can do Waking Up Practice on your own if you're an experienced reader. First, read the steps to yourself before you get in bed. Then turn off your light and use your imagination to follow the steps outlined in the exercise. If you're not an experienced reader, your coach can continue to read the steps to you before you go to sleep.

Even if you're a terrific reader, consider having your coach read the 10 steps to you once a week so you can concentrate on how your bladder feels when it fills up at night. (This is an optional part of the program, so you don't have to do it if you don't want to.)

Darrell's Story

I saw a 7-year-old a few years ago who came up with an interesting idea for his Waking Up Practice. Darrell wanted to do the exercise on his own, even though he was just learning to read. Instead of having his coach read the exercise to him at night, he asked his dad to record the 10 steps on a cassette. When Darrell got into bed, he played his dad's tape so he could concentrate on how his bladder would feel when it was trying to wake him up at night. He thought about the way his bladder filled up with urine when he slept. He thought about how his bladder would send a signal to his brain trying to wake him up. And he got up and practiced going to the bathroom to pee. The tape worked perfectly, and Darrell was proud of his ability to do things on his own. (**Coach's Tip:** Darrell's father recorded the steps twice in a row so Darrell wouldn't have to rewind the tape the second time he listened to the exercise.)

COACH'S CORNER

My 7-year-old does his Waking Up Practice, but he only wants to go to the bathroom once.

Because I want children to feel that this is *their* program, letting them play a role in setting things up is okay and may even increase their motivation to work hard.

So it's all right if your son simplifies the exercise. When you discuss this with him, it's not a victory for him and a loss for you; it's a negotiation where you made the program "fit" the child.

My daughter is afraid of the dark. Will this interfere with getting up at night to use the bathroom?

Fear of the dark and not wanting to get up when it's cold are the 2 most common reasons that children are reluctant to use the bathroom at night. I already discussed how to handle cold nights in "Tips & Tricks" on page 76. The best way to deal with fear of the dark is to use a night-light or leave a child's ceiling light on (a dimmer switch will enable you to lower the light intensity to a reasonable level). If adding light to the room isn't enough, consider the following options:

- Put a portable potty in your daughter's room while she's working on the program.
- Tell your daughter that she can call you at night if she needs someone to go with her to the bathroom. Although this is clearly inconvenient for parents, it's worth doing if it gives your daughter the confidence she's looking for to enable her to overcome her bedwetting.

CHAPTER 13

Bladder Exercises

By now you know that the bladder plays a big role in keeping kids dry at night. As a result, one of the things that will help you become dry is to exercise your bladder during the day. This chapter describes 2 exercises. The first one helps your bladder hold more urine. The second one helps you become more aware of your bladder signals when you need to pee.

Water Gulping

Over the years, I've learned that lots of kids don't drink much during the day. For example, many children skip breakfast and eat lunch without drinking more than a few sips of water or juice. One of the things that happens if you don't drink is you make less urine. And if you make less urine, your bladder may lose its ability to hold urine

HEY, COOL. WE GET TO DO SOME EXERCISES. I'LL LIFT WEIGHTS. I'LL DO SIT-UPS. I'LL RUN AROUND THE TRACK!

THAT'S NOT THE TYPE OF EXERCISE HE HAS IN MIND.

at night. Therefore, the best thing you can do to exercise your bladder is to drink more during the day. (I call this exercise Water Gulping.) By drinking more, your bladder fills up more often and you get more practice going to the bathroom to pee. Water Gulping also changes the way you drink. Many children drink most of their liquids at dinner or before bed. Water Gulping encourages you to drink earlier in the day. (If you normally drink a lot of liquids, you can skip this exercise.)

How to Do Water Gulping

1. Drink 2 extra glasses of water during the day.
2. Drink the first glass with lunch and the second glass when you come home from school. (If you usually have milk or juice with lunch, that can count as one of your drinks, as long as you finish it.)
3. If it's a nonschool day, drink the first glass with lunch and the second glass sometime before dinner.
4. Because it's hard to change the way you drink, it will help if you keep a Water Gulping Chart. One way to do this is to use the checklist in Appendix A. In addition, consider the following suggestions:
   - Put a reminder note (or a bottle of water) in your lunch box.
   - If you buy lunch at school, put a reminder note with your lunch money.
   - Leave a bottle of water on the kitchen table or other places you're likely to go when you first get home from school.
   - Have one of your coaches remind you to drink some water when you get home from school. (Your coaches should not do this unless you give them permission to remind you.)
   - Water is more enjoyable if you drink it with a salty snack like pretzels or crackers.
5. Continue the exercise as long as you're doing the program.

TEN SWALLOWS AT A WATER FOUNTAIN GIVES YOU ABOUT 4 OUNCES OF WATER. IF YOU FORGET TO DRINK WATER AT LUNCH, TRY TO GRAB A FEW GULPS AT RECESS OR SOME OTHER TIME DURING THE DAY.

Bladder Attention

I mentioned in Chapter 3 that the reason kids wet the bed is because their bladders and brains aren't talking to each other at night. One way to help this process is to think about your bladder signals during the day. If you pay close attention to these feelings, it may help your brain recognize them while you're sleeping. (I call this exercise Bladder Attention.)

How to Do Bladder Attention

1. As soon as you feel the urge to pee, stop what you're doing and go to the bathroom.
2. Think about how your stretching nerves are sending a signal to your brain, letting you know that it's time to pee.
3. Remind yourself that these are the same signals your bladder sends to your brain while you're sleeping.
4. Picture your bladder filling up like a balloon fills up with water.
5. When you get to the bathroom, imagine that your bladder is the size of an orange and concentrate on this picture as you start to pee.
6. Remember the "Tips & Tricks" in Chapter 8 on page 55 that make it easier for your bladder to let out all of your urine.

7. After you finish peeing, squeeze your sphincter muscle a couple of times. Remember that this is the muscle you use to hold in your urine.

8. Do this exercise 2 or more times per day. The best time to do it is in the morning before school or in the afternoon when you get home. On nonschool days, do it anytime you're home.

9. It will help you remember to do the exercise if you make a chart and record each time you do it. One way to do this is to use the checklist in Appendix A.

COACH'S CORNER

My 9-year-old drinks three 8-ounce glasses of water or juice every day. Does he need to do Water Gulping?

I mentioned under "Water Gulping" on page 82 that kids can skip this exercise if they drink a lot during the day. From what you've mentioned, it sounds like your son is drinking plenty of fluids on his own. Therefore, it's not necessary for him to add Water Gulping to the program. Give him a thumbs-up and tell him to keep up the good work.

My daughter doesn't want to do Water Gulping because it makes her urinate more during the day and she doesn't like using the bathroom at school.

I hear about this almost every day at work. Not the Water Gulping part, but children not wanting to use the bathroom at school. When I ask kids why they're reluctant to use the bathroom, here are the answers I get:

- "The toilet seats are wet."
- "There's no privacy."
- "It's too smelly."
- "The room is gross."
- "I just don't want to."

There are 2 ways to address your daughter's concerns. The first is trying to convince her to use the bathroom. The second is adjusting the program to fit her needs. The following is a list of some things she can do to make the bathroom experience more tolerable:

- Show her how adults use toilet paper to dry and cover toilet seats before they sit down.
- Show her how you can squat over a toilet to pee.
- Have her use the bathroom during class time when fewer kids are there. This may require a note for the teacher letting the school know that your daughter has a bladder problem.

If these ideas don't change your daughter's mind, you'll need to adjust the Water Gulping exercise. The obvious solution is to drink

continued on next page

COACH'S CORNER
continued

1 glass of water after school and 2 glasses per day on weekends and holidays.

My son has trouble doing his Bladder Attention exercise because he has a small bladder and needs to pee as soon as he feels the urge to go.

Children with small bladders often have little warning before they urinate, and when they get the urge to go, it's very strong and difficult to inhibit. (Kids with normal-sized bladders will have the same sensation if they wait until the last minute to go.) Tell your son not to worry if he doesn't have time to think about his bladder feelings. Have him focus on getting to the bathroom as soon as he feels the urge to go. He can then imagine his bladder getting smaller as he urinates.

CHAPTER 14

Contracts & Rewards

The purpose of this chapter is to explain why you sign a contract
before you begin the program and why I think it's a good idea to
give you rewards for the work you put into becoming dry at night.
The contract and types of rewards I'm referring to are described
in Chapter 21.

What Is a Contract?

A contract is an agreement between people that puts in writing
something they say they will do. It's very common for grown-ups
to sign contracts before they begin a project. For example, if
someone is painting your house or installing a new air conditioner,
your parents will sign a contract that says what's going to be done
and how much it will cost.

Why Do I Need to Sign a Contract Before Doing the Waking Up Dry Program?

A lot of kids aren't sure why they need to sign a contract before
they start using their alarm. We do this because the program lasts
a couple of months and it's easy to forget what you agreed to do
before you started. By putting things in a contract, you and your
coaches will know exactly what's expected during the program.
This makes it less likely that you will argue about things later on.

What Are Rewards?

My grandfather used to say that the best reward is the satisfaction one gets from accomplishing something. For example, let's say you've been practicing a new song on the piano for weeks. You practice for 30 minutes every day. In the beginning, you make lots of mistakes—either you hit the wrong keys or your timing is off and the song doesn't sound the way you want it to. Whenever you sit down to play, you get frustrated because your fingers won't do what you want them to do. Your parents and piano teacher encourage you and reassure you that you will master the song in time. In the beginning, you can't imagine that you will ever learn the song. However, by practicing day after day, you start making fewer mistakes and the song begins to sound more like the way you hear it in your head. After a few weeks, you not only play it without mistakes, but your piano teacher tells you it sounds terrific! In this instance, my grandfather was right—the best reward is the fact that you can play the song the way you want to. All of your hard work paid off, and you play the song with pride for your friends and family.

In reality, some of the things people need to do are not only harder than learning a song on the piano, but they take longer. And the longer it takes to master a skill, the more likely it is that they will lose interest and stop doing the hard work that's needed to be successful. Rewards are a way to get people to do things. For example, adults get paid when they go to work, and they appreciate it if someone gives them a bonus (extra money, more vacation) because they're doing a good job.

As a pediatrician, I recommend that children get rewards in many situations. I give kids rewards (usually a piece of candy) if they have to take medicine that tastes bad. I also give kids rewards (usually a sticker) if they pee or poop on the potty when they're being toilet trained. I don't give rewards for everything. For example, I wouldn't give someone a reward for making the bed or carrying dirty dishes to the sink. Rewards are given for situations that require extra effort.

What Types of Rewards Do I Get for Doing the Waking Up Dry Program?

Your coaches will give you a small reward once a week during the program. These rewards are for the effort you put into the program, *not* for dry nights. Once you finish the program, you will get a special reward that's like a "graduation present" for becoming dry.

Although rewards are an important way to recognize the effort you put into the program, don't forget that becoming dry is the best reward of all. When I see children for bedwetting visits, I ask them what they're looking forward to when they finish the program. Here are some of the answers I've received over the years. Put an X by each statement that applies to you and fill in the blank spaces if you can think of any others.

☐ I'll be able to go on sleepovers whenever I want to.

☐ I won't go to bed wondering if I'll be wet in the morning.

☐ My parents will be proud of me.

☐ I'll be proud of myself.

☐ I won't wake up in a cold, wet bed.

☐ I won't have to worry about someone finding out that I wet the bed.

☐ I'll be able to drink before bed if I want to.

☐ I won't feel like a little kid anymore.

☐ My parents won't have extra laundry to do.

☐ My room won't smell like urine.

☐ I won't have to wake up early to take care of my wet bed.

☐ I won't be embarrassed anymore.

☐ I won't have to worry that my brother or sister is going to tease me about wetting the bed.

☐ _____

☐ _____

☐ _____

☐ _____

☐ _____

☐ _____

☐ _____

☐ _____

☐ _____

☐ _____

☐ _____

COACH'S CORNER

I don't see why we should give our son something special just for becoming dry at night. Isn't that reward enough?

Like my grandfather, some parents think children should be motivated on their own without the need for rewards. Other parents equate rewards with bribes. On a practical level, however, they are very different. A bribe is something the child is given *before* he does what's expected of him. A reward is something the child gets *after* he carries out a task. In the former situation, the child is put in control and has the power to dawdle or refuse to hold up his end of the bargain. In the latter situation, the reward is a concrete way of saying "thank you" for a job well done. Despite the power of rewards, they are not an end in themselves. Rewards should always be paired with praise and encouragement. Together, they can make the difference between a cooperative and an uncooperative child. And as far as bedwetting goes, we know that rewards help.

My wife wants to give our 6-year-old daughter a piece of candy every time she has a dry bed.

I generally don't recommend giving a child candy every time she has a dry bed. What I prefer is setting up a reward calendar on which you give your child stickers or stars every time she has a dry night. Then, after she's been dry for a few days, you can, for example, give her some candy or let her pick a restaurant for dinner. I like this method because it recognizes the child's accomplishment, but also lets her appreciate the fact that she really worked for the reward.

I have a 13-year-old son with primary nighttime wetting. He's very enthusiastic about the program, but he doesn't want to use a contract and doesn't care about getting weekly rewards.

Most children like the weekly rewards for the reasons previously described. However, if your child is motivated and has a track record of sticking with things, it's okay to do the program without these psychological extras. Remind him that the program can get difficult at times, and discuss ways that you can be supportive if he gets discouraged.

CHAPTER 15

You Can Do It!

One of the things I mentioned at the beginning of the book is how important it is to practice when you're learning a new skill. When I see children in my office, I ask them if they have any heroes. Most kids answer this question by choosing a famous athlete. Others pick teachers, family members, or even famous people from the past. In each case, however, the person named is someone the child looks up to because of something that person accomplished in his or her life. For this discussion, let's say you picked a soccer player as the person you look up to. To be good at the sport, what do you think a soccer player has to do day after day? To help answer this question, I'll give you 3 choices.

1. Read about soccer.

2. Watch people play soccer.

3. Practice, practice, practice.

The correct answer is 3. If you want to be really good at soccer, you have to practice day after day. You have to practice when it's sunny outside and when it's rainy outside. You have to practice when you have lots of energy and when you're tired and would rather stay home. You have to practice when you're having a great day and everything is going right and on days when you're not playing very well. This is what it takes to be really good at soccer. This is also what is takes to be good at basketball, baseball, teaching, or even becoming dry at night.

There may be times during the program when you get really frustrated. You might not want to do your bladder exercises. You might get up late for school and not want to fill out your calendar. If you're using the bedwetting alarm, you might have lots of wet nights in the beginning, or you might be really tired from all the times you get woken up by the alarm. It's okay to be upset when this happens. Talk to your coach about it. Talk to your doctor or nurse practitioner about it. **But don't give up!** Remember what athletes have to do to be really good at something. The same thing applies to you when you're doing the Waking Up Dry Program.

There is one more thing you can do if you're discouraged about the program—think about all the goals you have accomplished in your life. Children have to learn a million things as they grow up, and it takes lots of practice to master these skills. Here's a list of things that most kids have to work hard at to master:

- Tying your shoes
- Throwing and catching a ball
- Riding a bike
- Reading and writing
- Going across the monkey bars
- Playing a musical instrument
- Swimming
- Burping whenever you want to (just kidding)

Because each of us is different, list some of your own accomplishments in the spaces below. Ask your coaches for help if you can't think of anything right away.

- _____

- _____

- _____

- _____

- _____

Have your coaches list some of the things they have accomplished in their lives, either as adults or kids. Ask them to tell you how hard it was to accomplish these goals and the frustrations they experienced along the way.

- _____

- _____

- _____

- _____

- _____

As you get ready to start your program, remember the things you read in this chapter. If you get frustrated once you're doing the program, come back and read the chapter again. **Remember— YOU CAN DO IT!**

PART 4

The Bedwetting Alarm

CHAPTER 16

The Bedwetting Alarm

The purpose of the next few chapters is to introduce you to the bedwetting alarm. I will show you how to set up the program in Chapter 20.

What Is the Bedwetting Alarm?

The bedwetting alarm is a device that teaches your brain to pay attention to your bladder while you're sleeping. Bedwetting alarms have 2 basic parts: (1) a wetness sensor that detects urine and (2) an alarm unit that buzzes after you wet the bed. Bedwetting alarms come in 3 styles: wearable alarms, wireless alarms, and bell-and-pad alarms (see Figure 1 on page 100).

- **Wearable alarms** are the most popular alarms used to treat bedwetting. Depending on the model you buy, the alarm unit attaches to different places on your body. In most cases, you attach it to your undershirt or pajama top near the shoulder area. The sensor attaches to your underpants and connects to the alarm unit with a cord.

- **Wireless alarms** use a separate alarm unit that is not worn on the body. The sensor attaches to your underpants and "connects" to the alarm unit with radio signals. This is similar to remote control cars that work without wires.

- **Bell-and-pad alarms** also have a sensor and an alarm unit, but you don't wear anything on your body. Instead, there is a sensor "pad" that goes underneath your bottom sheet and an alarm unit that is placed near your bed.

Figure 1
Bedwetting Alarms

Wearable alarms

Wireless alarms

Bell-and-pad alarms

How Does the Alarm Work?

The alarm's sensor has the ability to detect small amounts of moisture. When you wet at night, the urine in your underpants turns on the alarm, creating a loud sound. When the alarm goes off it wakes you up so you can go to the bathroom and finish peeing in the toilet. After weeks of hearing the alarm, your brain learns to pay attention to your full bladder signals and you wake up before wetting the bed. Over time, most kids stop waking up at night to pee. This happens because your bladder learns to hold all of your urine until morning.

Figure 2
Alarm Sensors

A. Sensor pad **B.** Wireless sensor **C.** Snap-type sensor **D.** Clip-type sensor

Some alarms also have the ability to vibrate when they go off. This is a helpful feature because some children are more likely to wake up if they feel a vibration at the same time that the alarm starts to buzz.

What Do These Sensors Look Like?

There are a number of bedwetting alarms currently available, and each one has its own type of sensor. The sensors used with some of these alarms are shown in Figure 2.

How Does Urine Set Off the Alarm?

When you attach the sensor to your underpants, the metal parts are not touching each other because the fabric separates them. When you pee, urine wets your underpants and the urine allows the metal parts to "connect" with each other. When this connection is completed, the alarm goes off.

What Does *Beating the Buzzer* Mean?

When you first start using the alarm, you won't wake up until
the buzzer goes off and your bed is wet. As you learn to respond to
the alarm more quickly, you will wake up before your bladder is
completely empty. *Beating the buzzer* means that you want to get
up before the alarm starts to buzz or as soon as possible after it
goes off. (Remember that your sphincter muscle is the muscle you
use to hold in your urine.)

Does the Alarm Work With Children Who Are Deep Sleepers?

When kids first use the alarm, they generally *do not* wake up when
it goes off. Therefore, in the beginning of the program, it's helpful
if one of your coaches sleeps in your room so you can be woken up
right away. After a couple of weeks, most kids learn to respond to
the alarm and your coach no longer needs to be in the room. It's
still important for your coaches to be involved, however, so I recommend using a monitor (or an intercom) so they can hear the alarm
if it goes off.

Does the Alarm Work Right Away?

Some kids begin having dry nights rather quickly, but most continue to wet the bed until they've been doing the program for a few weeks. Some kids become dry all of a sudden. Others continue to wet, but the size of the wet spot gets smaller and smaller until they start having dry nights. Here's a summary of what you can expect. (The time between one step and the next varies from child to child.)

1. At first, you may not hear the alarm, and you won't wake up until your coach gets you up. Your bed will be wet.

2. In a week or so, it becomes easier for your coach to wake you up, but your bed will still be wet.

3. In a couple of weeks, you will wake up when the alarm goes off or as soon as your coach calls your name. Your bed will probably still be wet, but the size of your spots may be smaller.

4. You begin waking up as soon as the alarm goes off, though some nights will go better than others. The bed may be wet or perhaps only your underpants will be wet.

5. You will wake up on your own every time the alarm goes off. Your underpants will be wet, but your bed will be dry.

6. You will wake up the instant the alarm goes off and your underpants will only be damp.

7. You will wake up before you wet the bed and your underpants will be dry.

8. Some kids continue waking up at night to go to the bathroom.

9. Most kids begin sleeping through the night, only now they are completely dry.

10. It's *normal* to have setbacks along the way, meaning that you may wet the bed after being dry for a week or more. As the program continues, this happens less often, until you're completely dry. If you get frustrated, reread Chapter 15.

How Long Does it Take to Become Completely Dry?

Most children become dry within 3 months of starting the program. Some do it sooner, and some aren't completely dry until they've been doing the program for 4 months.

Does the Bedwetting Alarm Work for Everyone?

If you stick with the program, your chances of becoming dry are excellent. There are a few reasons why the program doesn't work for everyone, however. Some kids lose interest if the program turns out to be harder than they expected, and this makes it more difficult to become dry. In other cases, something unexpected may occur at home that makes it harder to complete the program or do it correctly. (Remember that it's important to use your alarm *every* night.) Finally, some kids have more than one problem that's causing their wetting. If a child is a deep sleeper, has a small bladder, and wets many times a night, it takes a lot more effort to become dry. If you fall into this group, I recommend that you work on the program with your doctor or nurse practitioner because taking a medication with the alarm increases your chances for success.

WHY DID THE SORCERER FOLLOW HIS WIFE TO THE BATHROOM?

BECAUSE SHE HAD TO TAKE A WHIZ.

Do Kids Ever Start Wetting Again After They Become Dry?

If you start wetting again, we call it a *relapse.* Learning to be dry at night is a complicated process, and some children will have occasional wet nights for no obvious reason. Other times, kids might wet the bed because they are sick, tired, or worried about something, like moving to a new home or starting school. Having an occasional accident is not a big deal. I discuss relapses in more detail in Chapter 22.

COACH'S CORNER

Why is it important for children to wake up quickly after the alarm goes off?

Research shows that the sooner a child wakes up after the alarm goes off, the quicker she will become dry. Most children go to sleep before their parents, so you need to be prepared to get to their rooms quickly if the alarm goes off. It's okay to use a monitor to help you do this, but stay close by and try to get to the room as soon as possible after the alarms starts to buzz.

I have a bad back, so sleeping on the floor in my son's room will be difficult.

Although it's helpful for coaches to be nearby to ensure that their children wake up promptly, there are circumstances where this is impractical. In addition to bad backs, a coach may not sleep well on a cot or an air mattress. In such cases, sleeping in a child's room may be a big imposition. If you can't manage this, use an intercom and make an effort to get to his room as soon as possible after the alarm goes off.

Is it possible to get a shock from the alarm?

Most bedwetting alarms are battery-operated devices that run on a very small electrical charge. I've been using these products for 25 years and have never had a patient shocked or harmed in any way.

continued on next page

COACH'S CORNER
continued

Do bedwetting alarms require any maintenance?

Bedwetting alarms don't require much upkeep, but it's important to read the instructions that come with the device. If the battery gets low or the sensor develops a buildup of residual urine, it may cause false alarms or fail to work properly when a child wets at night. You can prevent these problems by setting off the alarm periodically and checking to see that it produces a loud sound.

Do we have to worry that the alarm's battery will die in the middle of the night?

Bedwetting alarms are unlikely to run out of power during normal use. It's possible that a low battery may cause the alarm to function erratically, however. The following situations are the ones most likely to run down the battery:

1. If no one wakes up and the alarm is on for an extended period of time
2. If you use a vibrating model, which requires more power to work
3. If your child does the program for a longer period of time or has a relapse and uses the original battery that came with the alarm

What percentage of children become dry using the bedwetting alarm?

Depending on the study one looks at, bedwetting alarms are successful 50% to 75% of the time. Programs that include other behavioral components are more effective. In my office, for example, 85% of children who use the alarm become dry within 4 months of starting the program. There are 3 things that contribute to this success.

1. The program attacks bedwetting from different angles.
2. I eliminate less motivated children before we start.
3. I'm not dealing with a referral population, which may contain a higher percentage of children who are difficult to treat.

Approximately 15% of my patients relapse after becoming dry. Most of these children become dry if they repeat the program.

CHAPTER 17

Choosing a Bedwetting Alarm

Which alarm you buy is a matter of personal preference. New models come out from time to time, so you can check with your doctor or nurse practitioner to see if there is a current product that will work better for you. The following list does not include every alarm, but it provides information on models that will satisfy most children's needs. I rated the alarms based on their effectiveness, ease of use, and cost. (I used a 1 to 4 scale, with 4 stars being the best.)

Malem (★★★★)

The Malem company makes a number of wearable alarms—buzzing only, buzzing and/or vibrating, and a model that lets you record your own sound. Malem alarms are lightweight and come

HOW DO YOU GET A GIRAFFE IN A BATHROOM?

OPEN THE DOOR AND LET IT IN.

I DON'T KNOW.

with a clip-on sensor that won't fall off during the night. A 2-step process turns off the alarm: first, you unhook the sensor; second, you push a button on the alarm unit. This method of turning off the alarm encourages you to wake up at night and makes it more difficult for you to accidentally turn it off while you're half asleep.

In addition to its regular alarms, Malem makes a bell-and-pad model (★★★) for children who don't want to wear an alarm on their bodies. This alarm has a number of useful features such as a wide range of sounds, a volume control switch, and an optional 49-foot extension sound unit that can go in your coach's bedroom.

WetiX 102 (★★½)

The WetiX alarm is the only wireless model currently sold in the United States. The sensor is inserted into a special pad that's placed inside your underwear. When the underpants get wet, the sensor signals the alarm unit, which has a very loud sound. The alarm unit consists of a small box that can be plugged into a wall outlet or run off a 9-volt battery. Make sure the alarm unit is out of reach so you have to get out of bed to turn it off. (**Coach's Tip:** Because the sensor is small and doesn't use wires, children may forget to remove it before putting their underpants in the laundry. Although the sensor is washable, running it through a washing machine may ruin it, and the warranty does not cover this type of damage.)

The WetiX alarm is a very good product when it's functioning well. However, I've had some complaints from parents that the device does not always go off in response to a wetting episode.

Wet-Stop 2 (★★½)

This is a wearable alarm that has a number of useful features. The alarm unit attaches to the shoulder area with a magnetic clasp or safety pin, depending on the user's preference. It has 2 switches so you can change the loudness and nature of the sound. The alarm uses a clip-on sensor that won't fall off during the night. However, because of the snug fit, most children will need help attaching and removing the sensor to and from their underpants. Pushing the volume switch to the off position stops the alarm.

SleepDry (★★½)

This a wearable alarm that produces a loud buzz. The alarm attaches to your shoulder area with metal snaps. Because of the snug fit, some children will need help pushing the snaps together. The sensor consists of metal snaps that attach to your underpants. (The snaps don't touch your skin because you wear 2 pairs of underpants to bed and the snaps attach to the outside pair.) The sensor snaps are easy to push together, and you turn the alarm off by pulling them apart. Although these snaps are easy to use, they may come undone during the night. There are a few things you can do to minimize this disadvantage (see "Coach's Corner" in Chapter 18 on page 117).

Wet Call (★★½)

The Wet Call is a bell-and-pad model for children who don't want to wear an alarm on their bodies. It has a 2-level volume control and is connected by a cord to a 19-inch by 24-inch sensor "pad." The alarm unit is attached to the bed with a Velcro strip and safety pins. The pad is placed underneath the bottom sheet by itself or on top of the sheet in a pillowcase.

Nytone (★★)

Instead of attaching to your shirt, this alarm is worn on your wrist like a big watch. The cord travels up your arm, through the armpit area of your shirt, and down into your underpants. Wearing an alarm on the wrist is a disadvantage for most kids, though I've had patients who like the idea of wearing something on their arm instead of the shoulder area. The Nytone sensor connects to your underpants with a clip that's similar to the SleepDry alarm and, therefore, has the potential of coming loose during the night. Because the Nytone is worn on the wrist, its sound may be muffled if the alarm goes off while your arm is underneath your blanket or pillow.

Potty Pager (★★)

This alarm consists of a rectangular box that's worn inside a child's underpants. The Potty Pager fits in the "fly" area of boy's snug-fitting underpants. When a child pees, the circuit is completed and the alarm vibrates. This alarm produces a strong vibration, but it has a number of drawbacks (see "Coach's Corner" in Chapter 22 on page 148). Despite its limitations, the Potty Pager may be useful for children who wake up easily and need an alarm that does not buzz.

COACH'S CORNER

What are the most important features to look for when we purchase an alarm for our son?

When I see children in my office, I show them display models for the alarms mentioned in this chapter. Although I let kids play a role in which model they choose, I have my own bias based on how well the alarms work. The most important thing is to pick a comfortable model that is reliable. A reliable alarm stays attached at night, encourages the child to wake up to turn it off, and buzzes when it's supposed to. In addition, because most children don't wake up by themselves at the beginning of the program, you need an alarm that buzzes so you'll be alerted when it goes off. This is why I generally do not recommend a vibrating-only alarm for my patients (see "Coach's Corner" in Chapter 22 on page 146).

Where can we buy bedwetting alarms?

Bedwetting alarms can be purchased directly from the manufacturer or from resellers. Two good resources are the Bedwetting Store and PottyMD, which carry a number of bedwetting supplies including alarms. I have included the current cost for each alarm (at the time of this printing), not including shipping and handling. Some insurance companies reimburse patients for the cost of bedwetting alarms. How much they pay depends on your deductible and the type of insurance you have. Get a prescription from your doctor or nurse practitioner that says "medical device" before filing a claim.

Bedwetting Store
PO Box 337
Olney, MD 20830-0337
800/214-9605
www.bedwettingstore.com

PottyMD
2216 White Ave
Knoxville, TN 37916
877/768-8963
www.pottymd.com

Malem Single Tone or 8-tone Alarm ($80)
Malem Ultimate Single Tone or 8-tone Vibrating Alarm ($90)
Malem Ultimate Plus Recording Alarm ($95)
Malem Ultimate Bedside Alarm ($170)
www.malem.co.uk
These products are manufactured in England and can be purchased from the manufacturer or Bedwetting Store.

WetiX 102 ($146)
Wetless Nights
6215 Oakdale Ave
Woodland Hills, CA 91367
818/887-4924
www.wetlessnights.com

continued on next page

COACH'S CORNER
continued

Wet-Stop 2 ($90)
PALCO Laboratories
8030 Soquel Ave
Suite 104
Santa Cruz, CA 95062
800/346-4488
www.wet-stop.com

Wet Call ($85)
Koregon Enterprises, Inc.
9735 SW Sunshine Ct
Suite 100
Beaverton, OR 97005
800/544-4240
www.nitetrain-r.com

SleepDry ($60)
StarChild/Labs
PO Box 404
Aptos, CA 95001-0404
800/346-7283
www.sleepdryalarm.com

Nytone ($70)
Nytone Inc.
2424 S 900 W
Salt Lake City, UT 84119
801/973-4090
www.nytone.com

Potty Pager ($70)
Ideas for Living, Inc.
1285 N Cedarbrook Rd
Boulder, CO 80304
800/497-6573
www.pottypager.com

CHAPTER 18

Getting Familiar With Your Alarm

Before you use your bedwetting alarm, you should become familiar with its parts. It's easier to practice attaching and unhooking the sensor if you use a pair of underpants that you're not wearing. After you do this a few times, go ahead and wet the sensor with water to make the alarm buzz. Listen to the sound for a few moments and then turn it off. Once you're able to connect the alarm and turn it off easily, practice again, only this time attach it to the underpants you're wearing. Wet the sensor again to see what it will be like when the alarm goes off for real.

When I teach children how to use the alarm in my office, they are usually fascinated with the sound and the way the sensor turns the alarm off and on. I hear from parents that kids often play with their alarms when they get them home. Although this is perfectly normal, keep in mind that pets, small children, and some adults are sensitive to loud sounds. Therefore, it's a good idea if you don't go overboard with this goofing around.

Before you use your alarm for the first time, you should have a practice session with your coach to rehearse what will happen at night. On the first practice run, I want you to pretend that you're too sleepy to wake up. This will give your coach a chance to try the Wake-up Drill. It also lets you see what coaches have to go through sometimes to wake their kids up at night. The alarm must continue to buzz until you "wake up" and turn it off yourself. On the second practice run, I want you to get up quickly so you can *beat the buzzer*. Waking up quickly and beating the buzzer is what you should shoot for every night.

READ THROUGH THESE STEPS WITH YOUR COACH BEFORE YOU DO THE PRACTICE SESSION. WHEN YOU DO THE FIRST PRACTICE RUN, DON'T "WAKE UP" UNTIL YOUR COACH GETS TO STEP 14 AND WALKS YOU AROUND THE ROOM.

Supplies You'll Need at Home

- A bedwetting alarm
- A wet washcloth

First Practice Run

1. Attach the alarm unit to your undershirt or other location.
2. Attach the sensor to your underpants.
3. Lie down and pretend you're asleep.
4. Your coach will drip some water on your underpants to set off the alarm.
5. When the alarm goes off, pretend you're still asleep.
6. Your coach will call your name and say the wake-up message. "Timmy, you need to wake up! Wake up, Timmy! Timmy, you can do it! You need to wake up and beat the buzzer if you want to have dry beds." (**Coach's Tip:** Your tone should be animated and encouraging.)
7. Don't wake up yet.
8. Your coach will gently shake your shoulders 3 or 4 times and repeat the wake-up message.

9. Pretend you're still asleep.

10. Your coach will now sit you up in bed and repeat the wake-up message.

11. Boy, are you sleepy! Don't wake up yet.

12. Your coach will wet your face 2 or 3 times with a washcloth and repeat the wake-up message.

13. You're a real zombie tonight! Don't wake up yet.

14. Your coach will repeat the wake-up message and walk you around the room. (Don't make it hard for your coach to get you out of bed.)

15. Now you can wake up.

16. Turn off the alarm and go to the bathroom as you will in the middle of the night.

17. Come back to your room, change your underpants, and reconnect your alarm.

Second Practice Run

1. The second session should proceed just like the first, except this time I want you to get up as soon as your coach calls your name.

2. Turn off the alarm and go to the bathroom like you will in the middle of the night.

3. Come back to your room, change your underpants, and reconnect your alarm.

Waking Up at Night

When you do the program for real, it helps if you're fully awake once the alarm goes off, because you're more likely to cooperate with your coaches if you are alert when you get up at night. This should go smoothly most of the time. On some nights, however, the alarm may go off when you're in such a deep sleep that a fire engine wouldn't wake you up (see "Coach's Corner" in Chapter 22 on pages 146 and 149).

FUN FACT Have you ever noticed that your urine smells funny after you eat asparagus? (What, kids eat asparagus??) This happens because asparagus has a chemical in it that creates a particular smell when it comes out in the urine. What's really interesting, however, is that some people don't know about this odor because the smell center in their brain doesn't recognize it. If you tell these people about "asparagus pee," they will think you're nuts! Now you can enlighten them.

Tips for Hooking Up Your Alarm

The way you attach the alarm depends on which one you buy. Each alarm comes with its own instructions and you should follow these guidelines carefully. However, I have learned a number of tips over the years that apply to most alarms.

1. The cord that attaches to your underpants is supposed to go *inside* your shirt or pajama top. If you don't like the way this feels, wear 2 shirts to bed and run the cord between them. If this makes you too hot, wear 1 shirt and secure the cord to the outside of your shirt with masking tape.

2. If the cord is too long, secure it to your shirt with masking tape.

3. Even though bedwetting alarms are light, they bother some kids because they occasionally make shirts sag. If this happens to you, wear tighter-fitting shirts or attach the alarm unit closer to your shoulder area.

4. Boys should attach the sensor to the front of their underpants and girls should attach it to the bottom of their underpants. This is important because you want the alarm to go off as soon as possible and urine comes out of boys in the front and girls between the legs.

5. It's important that clip- or snap-type sensors fit snugly, or they may come undone during the night.

6. Bedwetting alarms work best if they go off right after you pee. Therefore, you should always sleep in snug-fitting underpants instead of boxer-type underpants or pajama bottoms.

7. Alarms that attach to shirts with metal snaps will damage fabric over time. Therefore, don't wear the alarm with your favorite clothes. Alarms that attach to shirts with safety pins can stick your skin, so be careful when you put them on.

8. Children sometimes don't like the way sensors feel in their underwear. If you can't get used to this after a few days, wear a second pair of underpants inside the pair with the sensor.

9. Girls should not wear nightgowns to bed because this makes it harder to turn off the alarm.

10. If you don't like the idea of wearing an alarm on your upper body, consider a wireless model or one of the bell-and-pad alarms discussed in Chapter 17.

COACH'S CORNER

Are there circumstances when alarms don't go off the way they're supposed to?
The main reason alarms fail to go off is because they become disconnected during the night. This can occur for the following reasons:

• **A child removes the sensor after the alarm buzzes and goes back to sleep.** Sometimes kids rouse just enough to unhook the sensor, but then fall asleep instead of getting up and going to the bathroom. The best way to check for this is to sleep in a child's room so you can find out what happens after the alarm goes off. If a child disconnects the alarm in this fashion, wake her up every time it happens until she is getting up the way she's supposed to. (This problem is less likely to occur with a Malem or WetiX alarm.)

• **The sensor doesn't have a tight fit.** This can happen for 2 reasons—a child's underwear is too thick, or the sensor itself has "loosened up" over time. Girl's underwear is the usual culprit with the first problem because it often has a double layer of fabric in the crotch area. If you can't find thin underwear, cut away the inner layer of fabric. The second problem is most likely to occur with snap-on sensors (eg, SleepDry, Nytone). If you can't tighten the

continued on next page

COACH'S CORNER

continued

sensor, the manufacturer will probably send you a replacement free of charge.

• **The sensor becomes detached because the child is an active sleeper.** You can fix this problem by securing the sensor (or cord) to a child's bedclothes with a piece of 2-inch masking tape.

Are there other reasons why an alarm doesn't buzz when it's supposed to?

Sometimes alarms don't go off because the sensor is in the wrong place. Although boys usually pee in the front of their underpants and girls at the bottom, this is not always the case. If your child wakes up in a wet bed, check to see if the underpants are wet where the sensor is located. If not, reposition the sensor on subsequent nights.

Finally, an alarm may fail to go off because it's not working properly. This can occur because of a low battery, a sensor that needs to be cleaned, or a problem with the alarm itself. Call the manufacturer if the alarm continues to malfunction after you replace the battery and clean the sensor.

Do kids ever get false alarms when they're doing the program?

I don't see this very often, but there are a few reasons why you may experience false alarms.

• **Worn fabric.** If your child uses an alarm that snaps or clips to his underpants, the metal sensors may touch each other if there are tiny tears in the underpants or if the fabric is too thin. If this happens, the alarm will go off even though the underpants are dry. To fix this problem, examine your child's underpants carefully, and throw away the "bad" ones or put them in a special drawer so they're not used with the alarm.

• **Urine leakage.** There are 2 conditions that may result in a small amount of urine leaking into a child's underpants at night. The first condition occurs in girls. Sometimes when girls pee, a small amount of urine goes into the vagina instead of the toilet. If this happens, the urine can leak out when they're in bed and set off the alarm. Girls can fix this problem by separating their legs when they pee or by sitting on the toilet backwards (this keeps their legs apart, which prevents urine from getting into the vagina). The second condition occurs in boys who are not circumcised. Most uncircumcised boys do not pull their foreskin back when they pee. If urine gets trapped in the foreskin, it can also leak out when they're in bed and set off the alarm. Boys can fix this problem by pulling their foreskin back when they pee and shaking off any drops of urine that remain on the end of the penis.

- **Perspiration.** If a child sweats a lot at night, perspiration may wet the sensor and set off the alarm. You can fix this problem by making the room a little cooler or by having your child sleep with fewer blankets. If this doesn't work, your child can wear a second pair of underpants inside the pair with the sensor. If this doesn't stop the problem, try a different alarm.
- **Faulty alarm.** False alarms may also occur if the battery is low, the sensor needs to be cleaned, or the alarm isn't working properly.

CHAPTER 19

Using Your Alarm

The purpose of this chapter is to review everything you need to do to use your bedwetting alarm. Using the alarm may seem complicated at first, but after a couple of nights, you'll be handling it like a pro! And don't forget, your coach will be there to help you.

Because you will probably be woken up by the alarm, I recommend that you start the program on a Friday or Saturday night. That way you don't have to worry about getting up for school while you're adjusting to the program. If you sleep in a bunk bed, make sure you use the bottom bed. Finally, it's a good idea to finish all of your nighttime activities before you put on your alarm.

Getting Ready for Bed

1. Get ready for bed the way you normally do—change into your pajamas or nighttime underpants and brush your teeth.

2. Take out 2 extra sets of underpants, pajamas, sheets, and blankets before going to sleep so you don't have to hunt for them in the middle of the night. If you use disposable underpads, take out 2 of them, as well (see Chapter 26).

KID'S ALERT See page 183 in Chapter 26 for a tip that makes it easier to deal with wet beds in the middle of the night.

3. If you wet the bed, you'll need a place to put your wet under-pants and bedding. Most kids put this stuff in their bathroom. If you don't want your brothers or sisters to see your wet sheets, pick another spot. One option is to use a laundry basket or plastic pail that's kept in your coach's bathroom. Don't keep wet bedding in your bedroom because that will make the room smell like urine.

4. Turn on your night-light or another light so your room isn't completely dark. It helps if the hallway has a night-light in it, as well.

5. Put on your bedwetting alarm.

6. Do your Waking Up Practice.

7. Remind yourself that you are the boss of your bladder and that you are going to wake up quickly if you can't hold all of your urine until morning.

What to Do When the Alarm Goes Off

1. If your alarm goes off, you need to wake up right away and beat the buzzer. This means that you should squeeze your sphincter muscle quickly to hold back any urine that's still in your bladder.

2. If you don't wake up when the alarm goes off, your coach will do the Wake-up Drill to get you up.

3. Turn off your alarm as soon as you wake up. If you have trouble turning off the alarm, your coach can help, but you should be the one to turn it off.

IF YOUR ROOM IS MESSY, IT WILL BE HARDER TO GET TO THE BATHROOM IN THE MIDDLE OF THE NIGHT. SO TAKE A MOMENT BEFORE BEDTIME TO STRAIGHTEN THINGS UP.

Alice's Story

Alice is a 10-year-old girl who wet the bed about 4 nights a week. She did not want her little brother to know about her wetting because it bothered her that she was wet at night and he wasn't. After talking with Alice about her concern, we came up with the following solution: Alice's mom gave her and her brother some chores to do around the house. Her brother's chore was to set and clear the table at dinner. Alice's chore was to take the dirty clothes to the laundry room in the morning. Whenever she had an accident, Alice put her wet bedding in with the other clothes and carried the laundry basket to the basement. Alice was very proud of her ability to take care of this problem on her own.

4. Go to the bathroom and finish peeing in the toilet. If your bladder is empty, that's okay. You'll try to beat the buzzer tomorrow night.

5. Come back to your room and change into dry clothes.

6. If possible, help your coach remove the wet bedding and remake the bed. If you are too tired, your coach will do it for you.

7. Reconnect your bedwetting alarm.

8. Turn off your regular light and get into bed.

9. Feel your sheets and imagine waking up in a nice dry bed.

10. Remind yourself that you are the boss of your bladder and that you are going to wake up if you can't hold all of your urine until morning.

Your Morning Routine

What you do in the morning depends on whether you had a dry night.

1. Fill out your Waking Up Dry Calendar to record what happened during the night. Remember that your coaches need to agree with you about whether you had a dry or wet night. (See "Kid's Alert" in Chapter 7 on page 49 and Chapter 22 on page 143 for 2 comments on this process.)

2. If you had a dry night, put a sticker on your calendar or record *D* for dry in the space. If your underpants were wet but your bedding was dry, record *SW* for small wet on your calendar. If your underpants and bedding were wet, record *LW* for large wet on your calendar.

3. If you had a dry night, feel your sheets and think about how great it's going to be to have dry beds every night.

4. If you had a wet night, review what happened during the night and give yourself a thumbs-up for cooperating with the program.

5. Put your alarm and calendar in a drawer or other safe place so no one will find them by accident.

6. Get dressed and go to breakfast.

7. Remind yourself to do your bladder exercises during the day.

COACH'S CORNER

Do you have any final suggestions about the bedwetting alarm?

Here are a few tips to keep in mind before you start the program.

- Most children do not wake up when the alarm buzzes at the beginning of the program. Therefore, it's important that you're close by when it goes off. Because you obviously can't sit in your child's room until you go to sleep, put a monitor in the room and be ready to get there quickly if the alarm buzzes. Most children wet the bed within a few hours of going to sleep.
- Until your child demonstrates the ability to wake up when the alarm goes off, it's helpful if you sleep in his room so you can wake him up. In most cases, you will only have to do this for a week or two, but it's time well spent.
- Once your child is reliably waking up at night, you don't need to rush to his room immediately. It's still important that you get up, however, because most children need help (or supervision) after the alarm goes off.
- The most common reason that alarms don't work is because people use them incorrectly. Follow the manufacturer's instructions carefully, and use the alarm *every* night.
- When you review what happened during the night, praise your child for his cooperation with the program.

What should we do if our daughter doesn't get up when the alarm goes off?

It takes a lot of composure to handle a child who doesn't wake up while her alarm is blaring in the background. If you can't rouse your child with the Wake-up Drill, try to get her to the bathroom even if she's half asleep (remember that your tone should be positive and nothing will be gained by arguing). You should also be aware that children sometimes say mean things when they're sleepy that they won't remember in the morning. Stay calm if this happens, reminding yourself that fatigue is fueling your child's remarks. If your child doesn't get up after 5 minutes, turn off the alarm and let her go back to sleep. If this happens, you need to have a talk about the program in the morning. (Also, see "Coach's Corner" in Chapter 22 on pages 146 and 147.)

continued on next page

COACH'S CORNER
continued

My son doesn't want to help with his bedding if he wets the bed at night. Isn't this his responsibility?

It's okay to encourage kids to help out if they wet the bed at night, but they should *never* be forced to do this. Children are usually very tired when the alarm wakes them up (as are adults), and having to deal with a wet bed may sour their attitude toward the entire program. Try breaking down the process into smaller steps. For example, your son may be willing to remove his underpad or top sheet. This allows him to take some responsibility for cleaning up, but isn't as taxing as remaking the entire bed. And don't forget the tips on page 183 in Chapter 26 that makes it easier to deal with wet beds in the middle of the night.

PART 5

Putting the Program Together

CHAPTER 20

Setting Up the Program

When I work with kids in my office, we set up their programs at our second visit. Although some parts are important for everyone, I let them fine-tune the program if they want to. (*Fine-tuning the program* means you get to make some decisions about what you do.) Let's review each part of the program so you can set it up to fit your needs.

IF IT SEEMS LIKE A LOT OF WORK TO DO ALL THESE STEPS AT ONCE, START WITH YOUR WAKING UP DRY CALENDAR, WAKING UP PRACTICE, AND THE BEDWETTING ALARM.

YOU CAN ADD THE BLADDER EXERCISES AFTER YOU'VE BEEN DOING THE PROGRAM FOR A FEW DAYS.

1. **Waking Up Dry Calendar.** This is important for everyone. Fill out your calendar every morning as discussed under "Your Morning Routine" in Chapter 19 on page 123. Don't forget to put a check on your calendar if you wake up on your own when the alarm goes off.

2. **Waking Up Practice.** This is important for everyone. Do Waking Up Practice every night. Remember that you're supposed to make 2 trips to the bathroom each time you do the exercise.

3. **The bedwetting alarm.** This is the main part of the program. It's obviously important for everyone.

4. **Bladder exercises.** Water Gulping is the exercise I usually recommend at the beginning of the program. (Remember that you can skip this step if you already drink a lot during the day.) Although most children prefer this exercise as well, some kids don't like having to drink extra water during the day. Either it's too hard to remember, it interferes with their appetite, or they don't want to use the bathroom at school. (See "Coach's Corner" on page 85 in Chapter 13 for some tips on how you can make Water Gulping easier to do.) If it's too hard to do Water Gulping, you can do the Bladder Attention exercise instead.

5. **Picking a cheerleader.** This is discussed in the next section. Although cheerleaders can be very helpful, this is an optional part of the program. (*Optional* means that you don't have to do it if you don't want to.)

6. **Waking Up Dry Contract.** Most kids love this part of the program because using the contract lets you earn your weekly and special rewards (see Chapter 21).

Picking a Cheerleader

When I work with children in my office, I have 2 jobs. My first job is to teach them how to use the alarm. My second job is to be their cheerleader. I like to call my patients a few days into the program to find out how they're doing and answer any questions they may have. I let them know I'm proud of them and that I'm pleased with how hard they're working.

KID'S ALERT

I have included a section called "Tips for Cheerleaders" as Appendix E. You can photocopy or tear out this page and give it to your cheerleader so he or she knows the responsibilities that go with this important job.

Because you're doing the program with this book, I can't be there to call you on the phone. Therefore, we need someone to do this important job. Although your coaches will be delighted with your progress, I would like you to consider picking someone outside of the home to be your cheerleader. This can be a grandparent, an aunt or uncle, or a grown-up that is a close friend of the family. If you're doing the program with your doctor or nurse practitioner, he or she can act as your cheerleader, too. Your cheerleader should know all about the program and is there to make you feel better about what you're doing.

My cheerleader will be _____.

Finishing the Program

I mentioned earlier that I consider bedwetting to be "cured" when you've been dry for 14 nights in a row. Experience has taught me, however, that stopping the program right away increases your chances of having a relapse. (A *relapse* is when you start wetting the bed after you've been dry for a while.) Therefore, I suggest a "cooling down" period during which you stop the program gradually.

1. After you've been dry for 14 nights in a row, wear the alarm every other night for 2 more weeks. On the nights when you're not wearing the alarm, leave it on your night table so you can see it before you go to sleep. If you don't have a night table, put the alarm on a chair next to your bed. Remind yourself that you are the boss of your body and that you will wake up at night if you need to pee.

2. While you're wearing the alarm every other night, you can stop doing your bladder exercises and Waking Up Practice, but you should continue to use your calendar.

3. If you're dry every night during this 2-week period, the program is finished and it's time to get your special reward (see Chapter 21).

4. If you wet the bed during this 2-week period, restart the program.

5. When you've been dry for another 14 nights in a row, go back to step 1 and repeat the "cooling down" period.

6. If you start wetting again, add a technique called *overlearning* to the program (see page 144 in Chapter 22).

HEY, I'M GETTING THE HANG OF THIS.

COACH'S CORNER

My wife and I are getting ready to start the program with our daughter. Does one of us have to do everything?

Parents often ask how they should divide up their coaching responsibilities. There are lots of ways to work this out, though in most cases one parent acts as the head coach and the other parent helps out as needed. (The time when head coaches need the most help is when alarms go off in the middle of the night.) If there are 2 head coaches, you can alternate responsibilities from day to day.

My son has attention-deficit/hyperactivity disorder (ADHD), and I'm concerned that he won't be able to follow all the steps in your program.

If children have ADHD, learning disabilities, or certain psychological problems, the program may overwhelm them. When I run into this situation at work, I make things as easy as possible. One way to accomplish this is to concentrate on the bedwetting alarm and not bother with bladder exercises or Waking Up Practice. (I still recommend the calendar and contract.) If the child isn't making progress by the time he's 3 to 4 weeks into the program, I consider adding these other elements at that time.

My 7-year-old doesn't have ADHD, but I still think the program is too complicated for her.

Although I generally simplify the program only for the situations noted above, you can choose this option if you think the full program will be too much for your child. You can also simplify the program if your child becomes exhausted from being woken up by the alarm.

I bought your book for my 9-year-old son, but he doesn't want to read it.

Sometimes children have an approach/avoidance reaction when it comes to working on medical problems. If your son hasn't treated his bedwetting in the past, he may need a little time to get used to the idea. Give him a week to think about it and then talk to him again.

continued on next page

COACH'S CORNER
continued

If your son tried to become dry in the past and failed, it's natural that he'd react this way. This occurs because some people, especially children, find it safer to accept a problem than to risk failing again. The best thing to do is to leave the book in a nonpublic spot in your home. Tell your son he can look at the book if he wants to, but make it clear that it's up to him.

I would also tell him that looking at the book does not mean he has to do the program. Let him know that you're available to discuss the book any time he wants to. There's a reasonable chance that his interest may grow in a few weeks if you don't push the issue.

My 11-year-old has always wet the bed at night. One of my friends recently suggested that we take him to a specialist.

In most cases, your regular provider will be able to treat your child's wetting. However, if you're not getting the help you need in this setting, there are a few specialists that have an interest in bedwetting. Pediatric urologists are surgeons that specialize in the urinary tract. They're experts in bedwetting and spend a lot of their time helping children become dry. Urologists are particularly skilled helping children with complicated types of wetting. Pediatric nephrologists are pediatricians that specialize in kidney problems. They also know a lot about wetting problems.

One thing to keep in mind is that while urologists and nephrologists are very knowledgeable about bedwetting, some of them are more inclined to use medication than behavioral techniques with children. If you see a specialist, discuss the pros and cons of each approach so you can choose the one that's best for your child.

Do you have any final suggestions before families begin the program?

- Try to remain enthusiastic and encouraging as your child goes through the program.
- Praise your child for all of her accomplishments with the program, not just dry nights.
- Be sympathetic if your child gets discouraged. Listen first, then make suggestions. If possible, try to come up with solutions together.

- **Never** hold back weekly rewards because your child misbehaved in some other part of her life.
- Give your child help when she needs it, but let her take the lead whenever possible. Remind her that this is *her* program and she is the star of the show.
- If your child needs stickers for her calendar or some other attention concerning the program, stop what you're doing right away to demonstrate your interest in the program.
- Use gentle reminders if your child forgets to do parts of the program so she doesn't misinterpret your help as nagging.
- Finally, if you're feeling exhausted as you go through the program, remember this line by comedy writer Gene Perret: *Parenting requires patience, endurance, forgiveness, and understanding. And if the children aren't willing to do that, it's going to be tough.*

CHAPTER 21

Waking Up Dry Contract

The purpose of this chapter is to help you set up you own personal contract for the Waking Up Dry Program. Before we get to the contract, however, I want you to make some decisions about the rewards you'll get for doing the program.

Weekly Rewards

Here are some examples of the weekly rewards I recommend for the program. These are just examples, so feel free to come up with your own ideas. As a general rule, these rewards should take place on the weekend so they don't interfere with school or work schedules.

- Take a friend to the movies.
- Have a special outing with one of your coaches.
- Get an extra hour of TV or computer time.
- Do a special art project with one of your coaches.
- Go out for a special dessert.
- Get a small item like a pack of baseball cards.

You and your coaches must agree to the specific choices you make for these rewards. For example, if your parents don't allow you to watch certain types of movies, you can't choose them as rewards for the program. On the other hand, if you want to watch the same movie 3 weeks in a row, your coaches should agree to that request.

My choices for weekly rewards are the following:

1. _____

2. _____

3. _____

4. _____

5. _____

6. _____

7. _____

8. _____

Special Rewards

Here are some examples of special rewards you can choose for completing the program:

- A medium-sized toy like a Lego set or doll
- A sleeping bag
- A stuffed animal
- A dress or jacket
- A computer game or toy
- A piece of sports equipment like a tennis racket, basketball, or hockey stick

As with the weekly rewards, you and your coaches must agree to the specific choice you make for your special reward. For example, if your parents don't allow you to play with certain types of toys, you can't choose one of them as a reward for the program.

My special reward for completing the program is

- _____

Waking Up Dry Contract

1. I will begin my Waking Up Dry Program on _____ (date).

   My coaches for the program are _____

   _____.

   I agree to cooperate with my coaches until the program is done.

2. In addition to using the bedwetting alarm, I agree to add the following helper treatments to the program (check all that apply):

   ☐ Waking Up Dry Calendar

   ☐ Water Gulping

   ☐ Bladder Attention

   ☐ Waking Up Practice

   ☐ Cheerleader

3. I understand that being tired can make it harder to stay dry at night, so I agree to go to bed at a reasonable hour. On school nights, I will go to bed at _____ pm. On nonschool nights, I will go to bed at _____ pm.

4. Although my bedwetting is "cured" when I have had 14 dry nights in a row, the program is not finished until I complete the "cooling down" period described in Chapter 20.

5. I know it takes practice to become dry and the program may last 3 to 4 months. I also know that if I stick with the program, my chances of becoming dry are excellent. If I use a cheerleader, he or she will review my progress during the program and encourage me as we go along. My cheerleader for the program

   is _____.

6. I understand that my coaches are here to help me. They will read the book to me if I need assistance, and they will review the book with me as I do the program. Although my coaches will encourage and guide me, they promise not to nag. If we disagree about any part of the program, we will review the book together to figure out the best way to do things.

7. Because it takes work to become dry at night, my coaches will give me a reward once a week during the program. These rewards are for the effort I put into the program, *not* for dry nights. My coaches and I will choose these rewards before the program begins. In addition, I will get a special reward after I have completed the "cooling down" period and the program is finished. My coaches and I will agree to this reward before the program starts.

8. If the program turns out to be harder than I expected, my coaches will encourage me to continue. They will do this by praising me for all the work I've done and reminding me of the progress I've made. My coaches will not force me to complete the program if I choose to quit. If I decide to do the program in the future, they will be there to help me.

_____ (date)

_____ (your signature)

_____ (coach's signature)

_____ (coach's signature)

CHAPTER 22

Getting Past the Rough Spots

The purpose of this chapter is to solve some of the problems that may develop when you're doing the program. If you haven't started yet, you can skim the chapter or jump ahead to Chapter 23.

Wetting the Bed More Than Once Per Night

If your alarm goes off more than once per night, it can create 2 problems. First, you and your coaches will lose a lot of sleep. Second, you may become discouraged about the program. How you approach this situation depends on how many times the alarm goes off. If it goes off twice per night and you can handle the situation, continue with the program as before. If it goes off more than twice or you find yourself getting discouraged, consider the following options. (Once you begin responding to the program, you can stop these measures and go back to using the alarm the regular way.)

1. Pee 2 times before you go to sleep. Go to the bathroom 30 minutes before bed and then again when you do your Waking Up Practice.

2. Have your parents take you to the bathroom before they go to sleep. By emptying your bladder at 10:00 or 11:00 pm, you may reduce the number of times the alarm goes off.

3. Remove the alarm after it goes off for the second time. Although you may wake up in a wet bed, this is better than being exhausted at the beginning of the program.

4. Talk with your doctor or nurse practitioner about adding a medicine to the program. Depending on the size of your bladder, there are a few medications that may reduce the number of wettings per night.

Getting Sick During the Program

If you get a minor illness like a cold, you should continue with the program. If you develop something worse, it's okay to stop until you're well. You can use Pull-Ups during the illness if it makes you feel better or your morning routine easier.

Feeling Discouraged About the Program

Sometimes it feels like it's taking forever to start having dry nights. If you think this is happening, check your calendar to see if you're making progress. If you're not making progress, follow the suggestions in the next section. If you are making progress, remember what I said about learning a new skill—it takes time, patience, and practice for things to pay off.

The Child Who's Not Making Progress

You can measure progress with the program in 4 different ways:

- Waking up on your own when the alarm goes off
- Smaller wet spots
- Fewer wet episodes per night (Most children wet the bed once per night. If you wet the bed more frequently, you can use this to measure your progress.)
- More dry nights

The following options are for 2 groups of kids: (1) children who have made no progress 4 weeks into the program and (2) children who made some progress initially, but continue to have mostly wet nights 6 to 8 weeks into the program.

KID'S ALERT

Bedwetting alarms sometimes go off because of false alarms. (This means that the alarm went off even though you didn't wet the bed.) One of the reasons this may happen is because a child sweats a lot and his perspiration sets off the alarm. However, sometimes kids think sweat is the problem when they actually wet during the night. If your coach checks your underpants and it looks like urine, this counts as a small wet spot, not a false alarm.

1. If you didn't do Water Gulping when you began the program, try it now.
2. When you do Waking Up Practice, go to the bathroom 5 times instead of 2.
3. Talk to your doctor or nurse practitioner about adding a medicine to the program. There are a few medications that may help by reducing the number of wettings per night.
4. If none of these options work, continue with the program for another 8 weeks. If you're still not making progress, talk to your doctor or take a break and try the program again in 6 to 12 months.

Dealing With Relapses

Learning to become dry is complicated. As a result, some children will have occasional accidents after they have reached their goal of 14 dry nights in a row. What you do about the relapse depends on when it happens and how often you wet the bed.

1. If you have any wet nights during the "cooling down" period, restart the program as described in Chapter 20.

2. If you start having accidents after the program is over, what you do depends on how often you wet the bed.

   - If you wet the bed less than once a week, keep track of your wet and dry nights with the Waking Up Dry Calendar.

   - If you wet the bed once a week, use your calendar and restart your Waking Up Practice. If you stop having accidents, continue with this plan for 3 more weeks. If the wetting continues, follow the recommendations in the next step.

   - If you wet the bed more than once a week, restart the program. Once you have been dry for 14 nights in a row, add a technique called *overlearning*. Overlearning is a procedure that strengthens what you learn with the bedwetting alarm. The technique involves drinking a 6- to 8-ounce glass of water right before you go to sleep at night. In many cases, drinking this amount of water before bed causes you to start wetting again—this is normal, so don't let it discourage you. Continue to drink the water every night and use the alarm until you've been dry again for 14 nights in a row. Stop drinking the extra water and begin the "cooling down" period the same way you did with the regular program. When you finish the program this time, your chances of having another relapse are very low (see "Coach's Corner" on page 152).

A GOOD WAY TO THINK ABOUT OVERLEARNING IS TO IMAGINE FAMOUS ATHLETES WHO CONTINUE TO PRACTICE AFTER THE REST OF THEIR TEAMMATES HAVE GONE HOME. THAT'S WHAT OVERLEARNING IS— REALLY HARD WORK TO HELP YOU STAY DRY AT NIGHT!

COACH'S CORNER

My daughter has been using the alarm for 3 weeks. If she wakes up to pee when the alarm hasn't gone off, it's hard for her to re-hook the sensor by herself.

Children sometimes have difficulty getting the sensor back in place when they're sleepy. Most kids can avoid this problem by not unhooking the sensor in the first place. (It was actually a patient of mine who figured this out and told me about it.) There are 2 ways to accomplish this. The first involves pulling the bottom of the underpants to one side before urinating. After the child pees, she can wipe herself with one hand while she continues to hold her underpants out of the way. It's important that she wipes herself well so the alarm doesn't go off because urine leaks out of the vaginal area after she gets in bed. The second option involves carefully pulling down the underpants with the sensor still attached. As long as there is a little slack in the cord or the child leans forward, the sensor shouldn't come off during this maneuver.

My 9-year-old has been doing the program for 3 weeks, and she's not cooperating the way she was when we started.

If you suspect that your child isn't cooperating with the program, pay attention to what she's doing for a few days. If she's forgetting (or refusing) to do some of her work, talk to her in a non-accusatory manner so you can find out why she's reacting the way she is. Here are some reasons why a child may not be cooperating with the program:

- She may be distracted by schoolwork, sports, or other interests.
- She may be coming down with an illness.
- The program may be too complicated for her.
- She may be forgetful—this is especially true for children with attention-deficit/hyperactivity disorder (ADHD).
- She may be frustrated that the program isn't working fast enough.
- She may be tired from getting woken up at night by the alarm.

If the problem is related to school or something else going on in the child's life, address your child's concern and point out how it's interfering with the program. If the difficulty lies with the program itself, share your

continued on next page

COACH'S CORNER
continued

observations and try to solve the problem together. If the program is too complicated, simplify things by reducing the frequency of an exercise or eliminating it altogether. If your child is just forgetful, work out a plan for reminding her without nagging. Before you make any suggestions, however, give your child a chance to come up with an answer herself. For example, some kids like to be reminded verbally. Others respond better if you hand them a note or put a reminder in their room. If your child is frustrated or has lost confidence in the program, reread Chapter 15 together. Hopefully, a pep talk combined with an understanding coach will be enough to energize your child so she can continue to work on becoming dry at night.

My son has a hard time unhooking his alarm after it goes off.

Children sometimes have difficulty unhooking their bedwetting alarms at the beginning of the program. There are a few reasons why this may occur.

- Most children are sleepy when they're woken up and may be "all thumbs" in the first week or so that they're using the alarm.
- Some children grab the cord instead of the sensor. If this happens, the cord will bend, making it harder to detach the sensor.
- Some alarms are harder to turn off than others. The Malem alarms, which do an excellent job staying attached throughout the night, are also more difficult to turn off.

Encourage your son to practice turning off the alarm before he goes to sleep. (He should do this while he's under the covers with the light turned off to simulate what happens at night.) In most cases, his ability to turn off the alarm will improve with time. If he continues to have trouble, you can help him turn off the alarm by guiding him through the process.

My 9-year-old does not wake up when her alarm goes off.

This is common at the beginning of the program, which is why I recommend that a coach sleeps in the child's room for the first 2 weeks that you're using the alarm. Be sure to use the Wake-up Drill described in Chapter 9 on pages 60 to 62. Most kids begin waking up a week or two into the program. If your daughter doesn't wake up at that point, stay in her room for a few more weeks or consider using an alarm that vibrates as well as buzzes.

When my son's alarm goes off, it wakes up his brother.

Most children don't want to draw attention to their bedwetting; waking a family member doesn't help matters. There are a couple of things you can do to remedy this situation. If your children share a room, it may help if you separate them until the program is over. The child doing the program needs to remain in his own bed, but you can temporarily let your other son use a bed (or sleeping bag) somewhere else. If your children don't share a room, you can try something that makes the alarm less noticeable. Play a radio at a low volume in the second child's room or set the radio between stations to create white noise throughout the night. Finally, a vibrating alarm may be the answer, as long as it consistently wakes your first son when it goes off.

When my son's alarm goes off, it bothers our neighbors.

This is similar to the question just discussed, though the solution is trickier because it involves neighbors instead of family members. Sometimes you can solve the problem by having your child move to another bedroom. If another room isn't available, consider putting your son's mattress somewhere else in the apartment. If neither of these options is feasible, you can reduce the sound the alarm makes by putting a piece of tape over the speaker (it needs to be loud enough to wake your son). As previously noted, a vibrating alarm may also solve the problem.

My husband and I take turns being on duty if our daughter's alarm goes off at night. Lately, however, I find that I'm the one who gets up most of the time because he sleeps through the alarm.

If your schedules require that you share this responsibility, you'll need another solution if your husband keeps sleeping through the alarm. Here are some possible options.

- Put a baby monitor in your son's room and place the other unit, turned up high, right next to your husband. You can sleep with earplugs so you don't wake up when the alarm goes off.

continued on next page

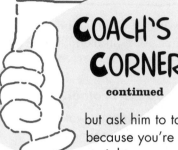

COACH'S CORNER
continued

• Have your husband sleep in your son's room when it's his turn to supervise. The alarm will be louder if he's in the room with your son.

• Let your husband sleep through the alarm, but ask him to take on other responsibilities around the house because you're focusing on helping your son when he gets up at night.

Do you ever recommend the Potty Pager?

In my experience, most kids don't choose this device when they see the other options currently available. Girls don't like the Potty Pager because they have to wear boy's underpants to use the alarm (it fits inside the "fly" area), and boys are sometimes hesitant to use it because the alarm vibrates against their testicles. The alarm also has a tendency to slide out of position during the night. In my opinion, the only reason to use this alarm is if you can't accommodate a buzzing model in your home *and* your child wakes up easily at night.

If you decide to use the Potty Pager, consider the following options to address these concerns:

- Have your child wear a second pair of underpants on top of the first. This may improve the snugness of the fit and keep the device in place.
- Sew Velcro to each side of the fly area. Once the alarm is in place, push the Velcro pieces together to reduce the possibility of the alarm shifting during the night.
- If you have a daughter, she may be more willing to use the alarm if she wears a pair of panties over the boy's underwear.

My 11-year-old has been using the alarm for 6 weeks and is now having dry nights half the time. Although he's cooperating with the program, he says he hates his alarm.

This is a common reaction in older children. When your son says he hates his alarm, what he probably means is that he hates the fact that he wets the bed and he resents having to do all this work to become dry at night. The alarm is a symbol for his problem and therefore is the focus of his frustration. Avoid the pitfall of saying something like, "How can you hate your alarm when it's helping you become dry?" Instead, say something that reads between the lines—"It must be frustrating to have to work so hard to be dry at night." This may open a channel for further discussion, or it may just let him know that you understand what he's going through.

My daughter has been using the bedwetting alarm for 3 weeks. I had to wake her up the first week, but now she's getting up on her own. You mentioned that it helps if kids are fully awake when using the alarm. Even though my daughter is doing what she's supposed to, I don't think she's completely conscious.

I like children to fully wake up because it makes it easier for them to do what's necessary after a wetting episode. However, I've been in the situation many times in which a child gets up and does what she's supposed to, but appears to be in a dreamy state. It appears that many children stop peeing when the alarm goes off even though they don't fully awaken.

My recommendation in this situation is practical—if your daughter is making progress with the program, continue as you are. If she's not making progress, rethink what you're doing. Go to her room as soon as the alarm goes off and try the following things to get her fully awake:

- Talk to your daughter with an animated tone, trying hard to get her to look you in the eye.
- Wet her face 2 or 3 times with a washcloth.
- Turn on the light.
- Turn on the radio or a CD player if one is available.

My daughter has a condition called tactile sensitivity and won't wear the bedwetting alarm. Is there another way to do the program?

Children with tactile sensitivity often react negatively to generally innocuous stimuli such as socks, tight-fitting clothes, belts, and foods with certain textures. Your daughter may be more comfortable with one of the bell-and-pad models. These alarms buzz in response to wetting the bed, but the child doesn't have to wear anything on her body.

continued on next page

COACH'S CORNER
continued

My son started the program 6 weeks ago. He's doing great so far, but we have an unexpected beach vacation coming up, and we're worried about what will happen while we're away.

It's not uncommon that vacations have a way of creeping into the program. The big question, of course, is whether you continue with the alarm while you're away. In general, it's a good idea to stick with the program if you can. One option is to have him wear Pull-Ups over his briefs. That way he can still use the alarm, but you'll have no clean up to do. Keep in mind that children are usually tired during vacations and it may be difficult to keep up with the rest of the program. Therefore, it's reasonable to limit him to the alarm and calendar to monitor his progress.

Our 10-year-old gets up when his alarm goes off, but he's very grumpy when we prompt him to go to the bathroom. He didn't do this when we did the Alarm Clock Test. Is he ready to use the bedwetting alarm?

I mentioned earlier that children sometimes lose interest in the program when they start waking up night after night. I don't think you need to stop the alarm at this juncture, however. Your son is irritable when he gets up at night, so it's possible that he's not fully awake. Try to wake him up using some of the techniques discussed previously. If you're unable to rouse him or he's still grumpy when he's fully awake, he may be overwhelmed with what he has to do in the middle of the night. Concentrate on getting him to the bathroom to finish peeing in the toilet. Help him put on dry clothes and reconnect the alarm. In the morning, compliment him on anything he did well the night before.

My husband and I have demanding jobs, so it's hard for us to get up night after night when our daughter's alarm goes off.

There's no denying that the bedwetting alarm is challenging for parents as well as children. Keep in mind that your fatigue will improve as your daughter starts having dry nights. However, if the alarm is too much of an intrusion given your current situation, consider the following options:

- Alternate responsibility for which parent helps your daughter at night.

- Postpone the program until the summer when most parents can slow down a bit at work.
- Encourage your daughter to do the modified program discussed under "Scoring Your Homework" in Chapter 11 on pages 72 and 73.
- Have your daughter use an alarm clock to get her up at night. She can set the clock to go off once or twice a night depending on her wetting pattern (see "Coach's Corner" in Chapter 10 on page 67 for a comment on the Wake Assure alarm clock).
- If your daughter responds to the medication desmopressin, you can use this on sleepovers and other circumstances when she needs to be dry.

My son has been doing a great job with the program, but he wet the bed last night after 12 dry nights in a row. He's pretty disappointed, and we're not sure how to handle it.

This is hard on kids, but it does happen sometimes. The key thing is acknowledging your child's feelings while trying to keep him motivated to stick with the program. Rather than repeat what I said in Chapter 15, I thought it would help if I wrote a mock dialogue that addresses your question. (I know that real life isn't this simple, but I hope it gives you an idea of how to approach the problem.)

Parent: What's the matter?

Child: I wet the bed last night.

Parent: You look disappointed.

Child: Wouldn't you be?

Parent: Sure I would. I'd feel lousy.

Child: When is this going to stop?

Parent: I'm not sure when you'll be dry for good, but I know you've been doing a great job with the program.

Child: Then how come I'm still wet?

Parent: Because it takes time to learn to be dry. Don't forget, you've been wet at night your whole life. Your body can't learn what it's supposed to do right away.

Child: I'm just so sick of it! When I wake up in a wet bed, I just think, "Oh no, not again. How can this be happening again?"

continued on next page

COACH'S CORNER
continued

Parent: Well, for one thing, it's not because you're not trying. Sometimes kids just don't wake up when they need to pee. Remember when I was learning to ski last year? I must have fallen down a hundred times before I got it right.

Child: I remember. Your nose was so sore, it looked like a strawberry. Come to think of it, I am waking up more on my own the past few weeks.

Parent: Exactly. You wake up all the time when the alarm goes off and lots of times when it doesn't. I'm really proud of how well you're doing.

Child: But I was so close to earning my special reward! Now it feels like it'll be months before I get it.

Parent: It may seem like forever, but it won't be. Hey, I've got an idea. Let's review all of the weekly rewards you've earned since you started the program.

Child: Okay. I'll get my calendar.

How should we act if our daughter has a relapse?

Having an occasional accident is nothing to worry about, and a calm and reassuring attitude on your part will help prevent your child from losing her confidence and sense of pride over her recent accomplishments. It also helps to remind your child of all the progress she's made during the program. If your daughter needs to restart the program, let her vent her frustrations for a while, and then try to bolster her motivation to work on the program again.

My 10-year-old has used the alarm twice in the past year, but she relapses every time we finish the program. We even tried overlearning, but nothing has kept her consistently dry.

This doesn't happen very often, but I occasionally see children who relapse after they do the overlearning procedure. I mentioned earlier that most kids who become dry with the alarm eventually learn to sleep until morning and don't need to wake up in the middle of the night to pee. Children who relapse over and over usually have small bladders and are not able to hold their urine until morning. When these children become dry, it's because the alarm teaches them to wake up when their bladders get full. Then, for some reason, they lose this skill weeks or months after the program is over. The only way these kids will stay dry is to consistently wake up when their bladders fill up at night. The first thing I'd recommend is for you to sit down with your daughter and encourage her to voice her frustrations about what's been happening. Once you have sympathized with her situation, there are a few options to consider.

- The next time you do the program, use the alarm until she's been dry for 30 nights in a row.
- *Hypnotherapy,* or medical hypnosis, is a technique that uses visualization, imagery, and posthypnotic suggestions to help people with many conditions (eg, to stop smoking, lose weight, and manage chronic pain). Hypnotherapy can also be used to treat bedwetting. It works by giving your child posthypnotic "suggestions" to awaken if her bladder fills up with urine during the night. If this sounds interesting to you, ask your doctor or nurse practitioner for the name of an appropriate therapist in your area.
- If all else fails, consider using a medication or have your daughter take a 6- to 12-month break from the program. During this time, institute a scheduled lifting program, with 1 or 2 awakenings per night to help her stay dry.

PART 6

Extra Stuff
for Kids

CHAPTER 23

Sleepovers

Children often ask me what they should do about sleepovers.
The answer to this question depends on several factors.

- Is the sleepover happening before or after you start the program?
- Do people outside the family know that you wet the bed?
- Do you want to go on sleepovers?
- Would you prefer not going on sleepovers?

One of the things I've noticed over the years is that children
sleep away from home at a much earlier age than in the past.
When I was a child, my friends and I didn't have sleepovers until
we were 10 or 11 years of age. Nowadays, kids sleep at their friend's
homes when they are as young as 5 or 6 years. Because bedwetting
improves as children get older, going on sleepovers at a younger
age means that more kids have to decide what they're going to do
about these events.

Sleepovers begin when children ask their friends to stay over on
Friday or Saturday nights. In time, kids start having slumber parties
at which as many as 10 friends sleep over at a time. The next type of
outing that children may get invited to are camping trips. They begin
as 1- or 2-night events with a friend's family. As kids get older, they
attend summer camps that may end with overnight trips. Children
also attend sleepaway camps that typically range from 1 to 4 weeks
away from home. For the purposes of this discussion, all of these
events can be grouped together under the heading *overnights.*

When Is the Overnight Taking Place?

Most likely you have already made some decisions about sleeping away from home. As you read the chapter, you can decide if what you've been doing works for you or whether you'd like to consider some other options. If you haven't gone on any overnights, consider finishing the program before sleeping away from home. Once you become dry, your confidence will go up and your first overnight should be a great success! Don't skip this chapter, however, because I include some tips on how to avoid going on overnights.

Do People Outside the Family Know That You Wet the Bed?

This is an important question because it lies at the heart of how you should approach overnights—if you're not worried about having a wet night at a friend's house, everything else is easy.

Some people think you should be open about your bedwetting. They believe that keeping it a secret adds to your embarrassment and that taking a "matter-of-fact" attitude can reduce these feelings. Most doctors take the opposite position—they worry that you may be teased if other people find out about your wetting. If you decide not to talk about your wetting outside the family, there is **no reason** for you to be ashamed about it. Always remember that bedwetting is a medical condition.

What to Do if You Don't Want to Go on Overnights

Do you remember how I mentioned in Chapter 1 that you're not the only one who wets the bed? I gave you this information not only to make you feel better, but also because it helps to know the facts. Well, guess what? Kids who wet at night are not the only ones who avoid sleepovers. As a doctor, this topic comes up with some of my other patients, as well. Here are some situations in which kids may prefer to sleep at home.

- **Eczema (EGG-ze-ma).** This is a condition that gives kids rashes on their skin. Children with eczema need to put medicine on their skin before going to bed, and they may not want their friends to see them when they have a rash or are covered with cream.

- **Sleepwalking.** This is a condition in which kids get up at night and walk around in a dreamlike state. They generally don't fall or get hurt, but it might be embarrassing to do this at a friend's house, and it could be dangerous in an unfamiliar setting.

- **Thumb sucking.** Most children stop thumb sucking by the time they're 6 years old. Some kids don't break the habit until they're older, and they may put their thumb in their mouth unintentionally after they fall asleep. If someone sees this, it could be very embarrassing.

- **Fear of the dark.** Some children are afraid of the dark, which makes going on sleepovers too scary.

- **Anxiety about leaving home.** Some kids don't like to be away from home. Either they miss their parents or they're just anxious (worried) when they are away. For these children, going on overnights causes a lot of distress.

If someone asks you to go on an overnight, you should have an answer ready so it won't look like you're fumbling around for an excuse. My favorite response is simple and direct—"I'd like to come, but my parents don't let me go on sleepovers." If your friend asks why they don't let you go, use either of the following responses:

- "When I go on sleepovers, I stay up late, which makes me very grumpy the next day."

- "I've got plans tomorrow and my parents told me I need to get a good night's sleep."

TRUE OR FALSE:
In the old days, doctors tasted urine to see if patients had a condition known as diabetes.

True
People with diabetes have extra sugar in their urine, and doctors used to make the diagnosis by tasting their patients' urine. Nowadays, we have machines that can do this for us. Thank heavens!

In my experience, this response works pretty well, and your friends should drop the matter quickly. If the invitation is for a slumber party, you can go to the party, but leave late in the evening before the other kids go to bed. For this to work, your parents should talk to your friend's mom or dad to find out when everyone is expected to go to sleep. That way your parents can pick you up as late as possible so you don't miss much. Your parents might even be able to bring you back in the morning so you can have breakfast with everyone.

There is one more thing you can do to feel connected with your friends even though you don't go on overnights—invite some kids to your house for "eatovers." These can be get-togethers where you have a few friends come over for a special kid-friendly meal. After you read my ideas, see if you can come up with some of your own.

- A backwards meal where you eat dessert first and the food last.
- A meal where you eat everything with your fingers.
- A breakfast where everyone comes in his or her pajamas.
- A "dog" meal where you eat everything without using your hands.
- A meal where dessert is a treasure hunt. Buy a bag of Halloween candy and hide it throughout the house. Tell your friends they can find the candy by following clues written on pieces of paper that each child picks out of a hat. Make it a cooperative game so no one wins or loses, but everyone works together.

- _____

- _____

- _____

- _____

- _____

- _____

- _____

What to Do if You Want to Go on Overnights

As I mentioned earlier, if you don't keep your bedwetting a secret, going on overnights is easy. Your parents should talk to your friend's mom or dad before the overnight so they know about your wetting. When you go on the overnight, you should use Pull-Ups to get a good night's sleep and make your morning routine easier.

If you decide to keep your bedwetting a secret, going on overnights is trickier, but you can definitely make it work.

Tips That Work for Any Type of Overnight

1. Try the medicine desmopressin before the overnight. If this keeps you consistently dry, you won't need to do anything else to make overnights a success.

2. Get a good night's sleep the night before you go away.

3. Try not to eat late into the evening and reduce your intake of liquids after dinner. This is different from my day-to-day advice (see "Drinking After Dinner" in Chapter 25 on page 174), but it makes sense to be extra careful when you sleep away from home. If possible, avoid salty food or drinks with caffeine that will increase the amount of urine you make at night.

4. Make sure you pee right before you go to sleep. When you're in the bathroom, take your time and empty your bladder completely.

Nathaniel's and Keisha's Stories

Although I generally advise my patients not to tell anyone about their bedwetting, I occasionally hear stories about children who don't keep it a secret.

- Nathaniel is a 7-year-old boy who went to a slumber party with one of my patients. There were 6 kids at the party and when they got ready for bed, Nathaniel said to everyone, "I wear Pull-Ups at night and I don't want anyone to tease me about it." Nathaniel was not timid or embarrassed when he said this to the other kids. No one teased him at the party or at school in the weeks that followed.

- A few years ago, I saw an 8-year-old girl for a bedwetting visit. When I asked Keisha if she kept her bedwetting a secret, she told me the only person outside the family who knew about it was her best friend Vanessa. When Keisha was 7, she and her mom had a discussion about whether it would be a good idea to tell anyone about her bedwetting. Keisha's mom was worried that kids might tease her if they found out about it. Then Keisha's mom had an idea. She realized that telling one person didn't mean they had to tell everyone. So Keisha's mom called Vanessa's mom and asked her if she thought it would be a good idea if the girls had a "secret telling" visit at which each girl shared a special secret with the other. Vanessa's mom loved the idea because Vanessa sucked her thumb at night and was afraid to go on sleepovers. So the girls went to lunch with their moms and afterwards they told each other their special secrets. The experience proved to be wonderful for both of them. They had sleepovers with each other after that and felt a special bond because each one knew something personal about the other.

TRUE OR FALSE:
Eating beets can turn urine pink or red.

True
However, this only happens to 1 out of 10 people, and the trait runs in families.

5. Kids usually bring sleeping bags to overnights. Sleep on the outside of the group so it's easier to get up and go to the bathroom if you need to.

6. If you use Pull-Ups, bring one for every night you'll be away, plus one extra in case something goes wrong. (I've heard of situations in which the elastic band breaks, making the Pull-Up unusable.)

7. Bring a sealable plastic bag for each Pull-Up you plan to use.

8. Consider telling a parent or camp counselor about your wetting in case you need some help during the night or in the morning after you wake up.

How to Use a Pull-Up in a Sleeping Bag

Children sleep in a variety of bedclothes at night—underpants, pajamas, nightgowns, and extra-long T-shirts. In the warmer months, children sometimes sleep in the same shorts they wore during the day. Whatever you decide to sleep in, choose clothing that fits loosely because it will hide your Pull-Up in case you need to get up at night. For boys, boxers hide Pull-Ups better than snug-fitting underpants. For girls, baggy pajama "shorts" or nightgowns do the job nicely.

There are many ways that you can use a Pull-Up in a sleeping bag. The following method works best if you have a place to change before you go to sleep:

1. Before you leave home, put a Pull-Up inside your shorts or boxers and place them at the bottom of your overnight bag. Put a plastic bag in your overnight bag as well.

2. When you get ready for bed, put on the Pull-Up when you go to the bathroom to brush your teeth.

3. Get in your sleeping bag as soon as you put on the Pull-Up. (If you goof around with your friends, someone may notice what you're wearing.)

4. Consider having an adult wake you up around 6:00 or 7:00 am so you can take care of the Pull-Up before the other kids wake up.

5. When you get up in the morning, take your overnight bag to the bathroom. Remove the Pull-Up, put it in a plastic bag, and close your overnight bag.

6. Get dressed and begin your day.

KID'S ALERT If you plan to sleep in a bed instead of a sleeping bag, put on the Pull-Up using the method just described.

The following method works best if you don't have a place to change before you go to sleep:

1. Put a Pull-Up inside a pair of underpants or pajama bottoms and place them at the bottom of your sleeping bag. Put a plastic bag in your sleeping bag as well.

2. When you're ready to go to sleep, get in your sleeping bag and wait 5 minutes or so for the bedtime chatter to quiet down.

3. Take off your underpants and push them to the side of your sleeping bag. Reach for your Pull-Up and slip it on with your boxers or pajama bottoms. If someone asks what you're doing, say you had an itch and were scratching your leg.

4. Consider having an adult wake you up around 6:00 or 7:00 am so you can take care of the Pull-Up before the other kids wake up.

TRUE OR FALSE: Urine is clean.

True
Unless you have a bladder infection, urine is *sterile* (which means that it's free of germs). Your mouth, on the other hand, is a cesspool of germs!

KID'S ALERT No matter what you wear to bed, make sure that you practice your sleeping bag technique before you go on your overnight.

5. After you wake up, remove the Pull-Up and put it in the plastic bag. Throw it away or push it to the bottom of your sleeping bag, whichever is easier to do. Put on your regular underpants and go to the bathroom to pee.

6. If you were dry, you can stay in your sleeping bag for a while before getting up. If you were wet, roll up your sleeping bag right away and tie it closed.

7. Get dressed and begin your day.

Additional Tips for Going on Overnights

1. Invite a friend to your house the first time you have a sleepover. This will give you more confidence because you'll be in the comfort of your own home.

2. The first time you have a sleepover at someone else's house, make sure it's one of your best friends. That way if something goes wrong, you're in a better position to explain what happened without being teased.

HERE'S ANOTHER IDEA FOR YOUR FIRST SLEEPOVER AWAY FROM HOME—INSTEAD OF GOING TO A FRIEND'S HOUSE, HAVE A PRACTICE SLEEPOVER WITH ONE OF YOUR RELATIVES.

3. When children go to weeklong sleep-away camps, they usually stay in cabins. Sometimes they sleep in beds, and sometimes they sleep in sleeping bags on wooden platforms. In many cases, there won't be a bathroom in the cabin, so be prepared to use an outhouse if necessary.

TRUE OR FALSE:
It takes a man longer to pee if someone is standing next to him at a urine stall.

True
It takes a man an extra 5 to 10 seconds to start his urine stream if someone is standing next to him in a public bathroom, and the closer the person is, the longer it takes for him to start to pee!

4. If you go to a weeklong camp, store the Pull-Ups in a pillowcase at the bottom of your overnight bag.

5. Going to sleepaway camp for more than a week is tricky because you need more Pull-Ups and there's a greater chance that someone will find out about your bedwetting. As a result, I usually recommend that you postpone longer periods away from home until you've become dry at night.

6. If you decide to go to sleepaway camp, one of your parents should talk to the camp director to find out if they have a policy for campers who are wet at night. Many camps make an extra effort to help kids with medical conditions.

WHAT'S THE BEST THING TO TAKE ON AN OVERNIGHT TO KEEP YOUR BEDWETTING A SECRET?

HARRY POTTER'S INVISIBILITY CLOAK.

CHAPTER 24

What to Do if Someone Discovers Your Supplies

It's important to keep your bedwetting supplies in a safe place so no one finds them and asks questions that may embarrass you. Mistakes do happen, however, so it's a good idea if you know what to say ahead of time.

This chapter describes situations that may occur while you're doing the program and ways you can handle them. There are no "right" answers, so fill in the blank spaces if you can think of any others.

Someone Finds Your Calendar

- "I've been exercising lately, and I'm using the calendar to follow my progress." (You can add that *LW* stands for long workout, *SW* stands for short workout, and *D* stands for day off. The check marks are for those days when you worked out extra hard.)

- _____

- _____

Someone Finds a Stack of Pull-Ups in Your Bathroom

- "They're my sister's."
- "My parents keep Pull-Ups on hand in case one of my cousins spends the night."

- _____

- _____

Someone Sees You in a Pull-Up

- "I have a bladder infection and my doctor told me to wear a Pull-Up because urine can leak at night with this type of infection."

- _____

- _____

David's Story

When kids see me for their yearly checkups, I usually ask for a urine specimen to make sure their kidneys are healthy. Sometimes the nurses give them a urine cup before the examination, and sometimes I give it to them after. One day I handed the cup to a 6-year-old boy while I was still talking to his mom. As we sat there finishing up, David pulled down his pants and started peeing right before our eyes! Lucky for me, his aim was pretty good and he didn't overflow the cup.

Someone Notices That You Were Wet at Night

• Same as previous answer.

• _____

• _____

Someone Sees an Underpad on Your Bed

• "I felt sick last night and my parents put this on the bed in case I threw up."

• _____

• _____

Someone Finds Your Alarm

• Wearable or wireless models: "I've been having trouble waking up in the morning and my parents bought a special buzzer to get me out of bed." (You can trigger the alarm to demonstrate how loud it is.)

- Bell-and-pad models: "My skin has been dry lately and the pad helps prevent rashes."

- _____

- _____

Someone Finds Your _Waking Up Dry_ Book

- "One of my cousins had a sleepover last week and left the book at my house by mistake."
- "Oh, that's an old book. I had some trouble staying dry at night when I was little."

- _____

- _____

CHAPTER 25

Lifting, Pull-Ups, & Other Measures

One of the things parents do to help kids stay dry is take them to the bathroom a few hours after they go to sleep. This technique is called *lifting* because in many cases, children barely wake up and walk "zombie-like" to the bathroom. (In some cases, parents even carry their kids to the bathroom.) Lifting is not a treatment for bed-wetting. Rather, it's a simple measure that parents can use until you become dry on your own or you are ready to start a bedwetting program. Lifting isn't for everyone, however. Some children wet the bed 2 or 3 times a night, and I usually don't recommend waking kids multiple times to keep them dry. Also, parents need to consider your age. In general, I think lifting is appropriate for children between 4 and 8 years. There are a few situations in which it's okay for older kids to use lifting as a method to stay dry, however.

- Sleepovers
- Vacation
- If circumstances make it impossible for you to do the Waking Up Dry Program
- As a temporary measure if you are setting off your alarm 2 or more times per night (see "Wetting the Bed More Than Once Per Night" in Chapter 22 on page 141)
- If you don't become dry after doing the program

Taylor's Story

A few years ago, one of my patients came up with a great idea for taking her son to the bathroom at night. Instead of just waking him, she used a combination of Waking Up Practice and the Wake-up Drill. As Taylor's mom got him out of bed, this is what she said: "Wake up, Taylor. Your bladder is trying to wake you up. Taylor, your bladder is as big as an orange and it's sending a signal to your brain telling you it's time to get up. You need to wake up if you want to have dry beds." Taylor's mom repeated this message as she tried to wake up her son. Some nights, Taylor's mom needed to shake his shoulders or sit him up on the side of the bed to get him to wake up. Other nights, he woke up right away. When Taylor walked to the bathroom, his mom continued to talk to him. "Great job, Taylor. Your bladder sent a signal to your brain waking you up and you're going to the bathroom to pee. You can do this every night if your bladder fills up with urine." After Taylor peed, his mom praised him for going to the bathroom and reminded him one more time that he would wake up if he needed to pee before morning.

Taylor's mom told me that her efforts paid off. After a few months, he began waking up on his own if he needed to pee in the middle of the night.

IF YOUR PARENTS WAKE YOU UP AT NIGHT TO PEE, IT HELPS IF YOU'RE AWAKE ENOUGH TO FIND THE BATHROOM ON YOUR OWN.

BEING AWAKE INCREASES THE CHANCES THAT YOU'LL BE ABLE TO DO THIS BY YOURSELF IN THE FUTURE.

FUN FACT The comedian Will Rogers once said that everything is funny as long as it happens to someone else. In that vein, I've heard lots of funny stories about lifting over the years. One of my patients was so sleepy one night when his parents woke him up that he peed in the garbage can instead of the toilet. Another patient fooled his parents one night when he looked like he was awake after they got him up to pee. He went to the bathroom, said goodnight, and then proceeded to get in bed with his sister. Fortunately, he was dry when he woke up the next morning. One of my female patients was taken to the bathroom at night, but no one noticed that she forgot to pull down her underpants until it was too late!

Pull-Ups

One of the questions that comes up at bedwetting visits is what children should do about Pull-Ups. My approach to Pull-Ups is practical. If you're a 5- to 7-year-old who's not ready to do the program, it's okay to wear them. Once you turn 8, however, you should stop using Pull-Ups even if you're not ready to do the program. Therefore, if you're older than 7 and you're not ready to work on the program, it's better to use underpads instead (see Chapter 26). There are a few situations in which it's okay for older children to wear Pull-Ups, however.

- Overnights
- During an illness
- On vacation if you're sleeping at a hotel or someone else's house
- If something very important is coming up, like a school play or special project, and you need to get a good night's sleep

Drinking After Dinner

Many people think that restricting fluids after dinner helps children stay dry. (*Restricting fluids* means that you don't take a drink even if you want to.) Although this helps some children, it doesn't work for most—if you limit fluids, you may wet the bed with 4 ounces of urine instead of 6, but you're still wet. Like Pull-Ups, my approach to restricting fluids is practical. If a child tells me that limiting fluids helps her stay dry, I give it my OK. Otherwise, I generally don't recommend this approach. There are 2 exceptions to this rule, however.

- If you go on a sleepover, it seems reasonable to do everything you can to be dry that night.

- If you take the medication desmopressin, it's important to limit how much you drink after dinner.

Word Search

```
W   A   K   I   N   G   U   P   P   R   A   C   T   I   C   E
S   P   W   M   Y   A   C   L   C   M   U   R   I   N   E   K
P   A   Q   O   X   B   H   D   K   B   O   I   D   G   F   Y
H   B   E   D   W   E   T   T   I   N   G   A   L   A   R   M
I   N   I   C   L   A   B   M   D   G   N   K   J   H   E   S
N   R   W   J   H   T   U   E   N   D   R   Y   B   E   D   L
C   P   Z   B   O   T   D   C   E   I   N   T   C   K   F   E
T   B   S   L   P   H   K   F   Y   E   L   X   O   Y   J   E
E   A   W   A   T   E   R   G   U   L   P   I   N   G   D   P
R   I   Y   D   N   B   W   V   M   P   F   J   T   C   Z   O
M   F   X   D   O   U   Q   G   R   E   W   A   R   D   S   V
U   J   V   E   K   Z   D   R   J   I   T   G   A   S   Q   E
S   A   U   R   T   Z   V   L   M   S   N   U   C   R   G   R
C   K   C   A   L   E   N   D   A   R   V   E   T   U   W   S
L   T   L   N   V   R   S   B   T   V   Q   R   W   I   Y   R
E   M   B   U   O   S   Y   O   U   C   A   N   D   O   I   T
```

BEAT THE BUZZER	REWARDS
BEDWETTING ALARM	SLEEPOVERS
BLADDER	SPHINCTER MUSCLE
CALENDAR	URINE
CONTRACT	WAKING UP PRACTICE
DRY BED	WATER GULPING
KIDNEY	YOU CAN DO IT

(The solution is on page 177.)

COACH'S CORNER

Do all doctors think lifting is an acceptable option for children?

Some bedwetting experts discourage lifting because they think it interferes with a child's ability to become dry by "training her" to pee at the same time every night. I disagree with this opinion for the following reason—because specialists only treat patients who continue to wet the bed, they never see cases where lifting helped. My experience is different. I'm a pediatrician, so I see the whole range of children's wetting problems, including cases in which lifting was useful.

Does my child have to be fully awake when we take him to the bathroom at night?

No one has studied this issue scientifically. On the one hand, it seems intuitive that becoming fully conscious would help a child learn to wake up on his own in the future. However, because many children are deep sleepers, it may be difficult to accomplish this. As always, I take a practical approach to the problem.

- If you can't fully awaken your child, help him out of bed, but encourage him to find the bathroom on his own. Stay close by to ensure that he makes it to and from the bathroom safely.
- If your child resists your efforts, do not force him to get up. Try again in 15 minutes or follow the tips under "Coach's Corner" in Chapter 22 on page 149 to see if you can rouse him enough to cooperate. If this doesn't work, let him stay asleep.

When I take my 8-year-old to the bathroom at night, she doesn't always urinate.

When children go to the bathroom at night, sometimes they just sit there and nothing comes out. If this happens, encourage your child to sit on the toilet for a few minutes before you assume that she can't go. It also helps to turn on the faucet because running water often stimulates children to pee.

Why do you recommend getting rid of Pull-Ups when a child turns 8?

I make this recommendation because I think Pull-Ups may prolong the time it takes to become dry at night. Although no one has researched this question, I've had some experience over the years that supports this opinion. For example, I've had a number of patients who became dry months after they stop using Pull-Ups. I've also had patients who did not become motivated to work on the program until they stopped wearing Pull-Ups.

Word Search Solution

W	A	K	I	N	G	U	P	P	R	A	C	T	I	C	E
S	P	W	M	Y	A	C	L	C	M	U	R	I	N	E	K
P	A	Q	O	X	B	H	D	K	B	O	I	D	G	F	Y
H	B	E	D	W	E	T	T	I	N	G	A	L	A	R	M
I	N	I	C	L	A	B	M	D	G	N	K	J	H	E	S
N	R	W	J	H	T	U	E	N	D	R	Y	B	E	D	L
C	P	Z	B	O	T	D	C	E	I	N	T	C	K	F	E
T	B	S	L	P	H	K	F	Y	E	L	X	O	Y	J	E
E	A	W	A	T	E	R	G	U	L	P	I	N	G	D	P
R	I	Y	D	N	B	W	V	M	P	F	J	T	C	Z	O
M	F	X	D	O	U	Q	G	R	E	W	A	R	D	S	V
U	J	V	E	K	Z	D	R	J	I	T	G	A	S	Q	E
S	A	U	R	T	Z	V	L	M	S	N	U	C	R	G	R
C	K	C	A	L	E	N	D	A	R	V	E	T	U	W	S
L	T	L	N	V	R	S	B	T	V	Q	R	W	I	Y	R
E	M	B	U	O	S	Y	O	U	C	A	N	D	O	I	T

PART 7

Extra Stuff for Parents

CHAPTER 26

Tips for Dealing With Wet Beds

For most children, the best thing about becoming dry is no longer having to wake up in a wet bed. The second best thing is being able to go on sleepovers without worrying about what will happen during the night. Because it takes time for the program to work, you and your child will need to deal with wet beds for a while longer. The purpose of this chapter is to teach you some practical tips that will make your morning routine easier. Although you're probably doing some of these things already, there are 4 areas I want to review.

- Protecting your child's mattress and pillow
- Making it easier to deal with wet bedding
- Getting rid of unpleasant urine smells in your child's room
- Supplies to have on hand

Protecting Your Child's Mattress and Pillow

When a child wets the bed, urine can leak through the sheets and into the mattress. Over time, the mattress will start to smell like urine. To prevent this from happening, you should protect your child's mattress with a waterproof cover. Mattress covers protect the top and sides of the mattress or encase it completely. Pillows are less likely to get wet at night, but washable pillows and waterproof pillow covers are also available. You can buy mattress and pillow covers at department stores or from medical supply companies that sell bedwetting products. Cheap mattress covers may crack or leak, so try to find one that's well made.

Making it Easier to Deal With Wet Bedding

One way to make your mornings easier is to put a protective pad on your child's sheets. These products, called *underpads,* come in 2 basic styles—reusable and disposable. Reusable underpads have cloth on one side and a waterproof backing on the other. Disposable underpads have absorbent material on one side and a thin plastic layer on the other. The reusable type costs more to begin with, but they're less expensive over time because you wash them over and over. Disposable underpads are more expensive over time because they're made to be used once and thrown away. Although they cost more, disposable underpads are easier to use because you don't have to wash them.

Disposable underpads come in different sizes and thicknesses. There are 3 basic sizes you will find—23 x 36 inches, 30 x 30 inches, and 30 x 36 inches. The advantage of the bigger sizes is that they cover a larger area, so your child is less likely to "miss" the pad if he tosses and turns while he sleeps. Which thickness to buy is a matter of personal preference. Thinner pads (light absorbency) cost less and will do the job for most children. If your child produces more urine at night, you can always move up to a thicker pad (moderate or heavy absorbency).

Some disposable underpads come with an adhesive strip on the back to keep them in place at night. Another brand, called Tuckables, have extra-long plastic "wings" that are tucked under the mattress. (Tuckables are 70 inches wide, but the extra length is in the wings, not the pad.) In my experience, most children are too active at night for any underpad to stay put. Fortunately, there is a solution to this problem. After you place the underpad in the correct spot, secure it to the bed with 4 lengths of 2-inch masking tape. (If possible, encourage your child to help with this step.)

TIPS & TRICKS

- Masking tape sticks better to flannel sheets than to regular sheets.
- If your child has a dry night, you don't need to change her underpad in the morning. In fact, if she has a run of dry nights, most underpads can be used for a week or so. After that, the absorbent layer gets tattered and needs to be changed. (Remind your child to make her bed every morning so no one sees the underpad.)
- The mother of one of my patients came up with a great solution to reduce her workload at night—she put 2 layers of sheets and disposable underpads on the bed when her son went to sleep. Then, if he wet the bed, she removed the top underpad and sheet but still had the second layer in place. Although she occasionally needed to put a dry blanket on the bed, this approach lets everyone get back to sleep with much less work.

Underpads are sold in most pharmacies and by medical supply companies that carry "incontinence" products. Medical supply companies usually have a bigger selection and are less expensive because you buy things in bulk. Pharmacies have the advantage of being close to home.

Getting Rid of Unpleasant Urine Smells in Your Child's Room

Bedrooms can pick up a urine smell even if you take care of wet beds right away. Therefore, it's a good idea to have a backup plan in case you need it. The easiest way to handle any odor is with room freshener. There are many types available, but they all work by putting a pleasant smell in the air. You can buy room freshener at pharmacies and grocery stores.

FUN FACT (for kids and coaches)

Have you ever noticed that when dogs go for a walk, they smell everything in sight? The interesting thing is, they don't smell for fun. It turns out that a dog's sense of smell is thousands of times better than ours. Dogs not only detect smells that we miss, but they use their sense of smell to identify things. As far as humans go, dogs recognize us by the way our skin smells. When it comes to other dogs, however, they rely on the smell of urine or poop. (That's why dogs spend so much time checking out each other's hindquarters.) So when your pooch is sniffing outside, he is actually checking out which dogs have been in the neighborhood lately. My daughter came up with a great term to describe this behavior. She says that dogs are checking their "p-mail."

Cats have a good sense of smell too, though you may have an extra problem on your hands if you own a cat. For some reason, cats will sometimes pee in the house if they notice another urine smell. Cats are territorial animals, so they probably pee on top of old urine to "mark" the territory with their own scent. The bottom line is this—if you have a cat, make sure to use an odor eliminator to get rid of urine smells on your mattress or carpet.

Another way to handle urine smells is to use a product that eliminates odors instead of masking them. These products come as sprays and solid odor absorbers and are available from medical supply companies. A great option for getting urine smells out of carpets is a product called Petastic, which is sold in pet stores. Although it's made for eliminating cat and dog smells, it works for people odors, as well.

Supplies to Have on Hand

The program will run more smoothly if you always have plenty of basic supplies on hand. These include disposable products as well as clean undergarments and sheets. Here is a list of things you'll need:

- Mattress and pillow covers (most children don't need pillow covers)
- Sheets, blankets, comforters
- Underpants

- Undershirts or pajama tops
- Pillowcases
- Underpads
- Two-inch masking tape
- Pull-Ups (for younger children and special circumstances)
- Odor eliminators
- Wipes (These come in handy when a bottom needs to be cleaned and your child doesn't have time for a morning bath or shower.)

Medical Supply Companies

Except for PottyMD and the Bedwetting Store, the companies listed here don't use the term *bedwetting* on their Web sites. To find underpads and other supplies, look under the heading *incontinence*. Also keep in mind that product lines change from time to time, and companies don't necessarily put all of their products on their Web sites. Therefore, it's a good idea to speak with a customer service representative to find the product that best fits your needs.

PottyMD (underpads and mattress covers)
2216 White Ave
Knoxville, TN 37916
877/768-8963
www.pottymd.com

Bedwetting Store (underpads, mattress and pillow covers, odor eliminators)
PO Box 337
Olney, MD 20830-0337
800/214-9605
www.bedwettingstore.com

HDIS, Inc. (underpads, mattress covers, odor eliminators)
9385 Dielman Industrial Dr
Olivette, MO 63132
800/269-4663
www.hdis.com

PaperPak (underpads)
PO Box 3240
545 W Terrace Dr
San Dimas, CA 91773
800/428-8363
www.paperpak.com
Note: PaperPak is a wholesale manufacturer that produces a wide range of underpads. Although PaperPak does not sell directly to the public, its Web site has links to many retail suppliers.

Incontinent Supplies Xpress, Inc. (underpads)
PO Box 480
Island Park, NY 11558
800/982-4199
www.isxprs.com

KCK Medical (underpads, mattress covers, odor eliminators)
14941 Calvert St
Van Nuys, CA 91411
888/880-1967
www.kckmedical.com

FUN FACT Have you ever seen a kidney bean? Most kids don't like beans and go to great lengths to avoid eating them. But how about chili? Along with beef and tomato sauce, kidney beans are one of the main ingredients in chili. Kidney beans are about a half an inch long and pushed in on one side just like a kidney (see page 9 in Chapter 2). So which was named first, kidneys or kidney beans? The answer is the kidney. Believe it or not, the kidney was first named about 700 years ago. The kidney bean got its name 250 years later because someone noticed that it looked a lot like the kidney.

CHAPTER 27

Medication

There are a few medications that doctors use to treat bedwetting. Although the goal of this book is to address the problem without drugs, medication sometimes plays a role in helping children become dry at night. Therefore, I thought it would be useful to provide some information about these treatments.

Desmopressin (Brand name: DDAVP)

The pituitary gland releases a hormone at night called *vasopressin* (VASE-oh-PRESS-in) that reduces the amount of urine the kidneys make. (It does this by reabsorbing water from the urine back into the bloodstream.) Although the research in this area is inconclusive, it appears that some children wet the bed because they don't make enough of this chemical. Desmopressin is a manufactured form of vasopressin that corrects this imbalance. The drug helps 50% of children who take it, though research suggests that it's less effective in patients who have small bladders. The effects of desmopressin are not long lasting and children usually relapse when the drug is stopped. For this reason, doctors generally recommend it for short-term use, eg, sleepovers, vacations, or special occasions. Desmopressin is also useful if children are not making progress with the program (see Chapter 22). Finally, a 6-month course of desmopressin is worth considering in children who don't become dry with the bedwetting alarm, but need some treatment that will get their wetting under control. (Recent research suggests that it's safe to use desmopressin for longer periods of time.)

Although desmopressin does not cure bedwetting, it's a safe medication when used as directed. That said, the following concerns should be noted:

- There is a small risk that desmopressin will lower the sodium (salt) in a child's blood which, in rare cases, can cause a seizure. This risk is greatly reduced if you limit a child's fluid intake on nights when he takes the medication. (Early symptoms of low sodium include headache, irritability, nausea, and vomiting.)

- Your child can have a 6- to 8-ounce glass of liquid after dinner, but he should avoid drinking more than a few sips within 2 hours of bedtime.

- If your child has an illness that requires extra fluid, stop the desmopressin until he is well. Also, withhold the medication if your child is doing the overlearning technique or has an unusually large fluid intake during the day.

- If your child is impulsive, make sure he doesn't drink water without your knowledge.

- Desmopressin is not a treatment for daytime wetting and therefore should never be used to correct this condition.

Oxybutynin (Brand name: Ditropan)

Oxybutynin is usually prescribed for patients with an overactive bladder. People with an overactive bladder get uncontrolled bladder contractions that cause frequent urination and an urgent need to empty their bladders without much warning. Children with this problem have a small bladder capacity and often wet their beds more than once a night (many children with an overactive bladder have daytime accidents, as well). Oxybutynin is not an effective treatment for bedwetting by itself. However, when used in conjunction with the bedwetting alarm, it may relax the bladder enough to make the alarm more successful. Therefore, if your child has these symptoms, talk with your doctor before starting the program or, alternatively, if you're not making progress by the time you are 4 weeks into treatment.

Although oxybutynin is generally a safe medication, like any drug, there are possible adverse effects. The most common side effects are dry mouth and facial flushing. Less frequent side effects include abdominal pain, constipation, and irritability.

Imipramine (Brand name: Tofranil)

Imipramine was originally developed as a treatment for depression, but doctors discovered that people who took the drug sometimes had trouble emptying their bladders. This gave someone the idea that it might work with bedwetting. Recent studies suggest that imipramine may also affect a child's sleep, making her more aware of her bladder signals at night. Although the drug helps 40% of children who wet the bed, most relapse once the medication is stopped. More importantly, the difference between therapeutic and dangerous levels in the blood is small. As a result, many doctors (me included) are concerned that imipramine isn't safe enough to use in a benign condition such as bedwetting. Doctors that prescribe imipramine do not generally consider it a first-line treatment and only use it if other approaches fail.

Patient's Story

Many years ago, I read about an 8-year-old boy who died after taking an overdose of imipramine. No one knew exactly what happened, but it was assumed that he took the overdose in an attempt to cure his bedwetting once and for all.

If anyone prescribes imipramine or any other medication for your child, be sure to tell him that it is very dangerous to take more than what the doctor ordered. You should also lock it up so it doesn't get into the hands of small children.

CHAPTER 28

Bedwetting Treatment According to Age

The following table summarizes which aspects of the program are appropriate for children at different ages. The word "yes" does not mean that you're obligated to do that part of the program, as there are other factors that will determine how you proceed. "Yes" simply means that a particular task is suitable for someone that age. The word "maybe" implies that it may or may not be a good idea to do that part of the program, so you need to individualize for your particular child. For example, few 6-year-olds are good candidates for the bedwetting alarm. Nevertheless, I have used the alarm with kids this age, so there is no reason to prevent a highly motivated child from using it.

WHY DID THE PRINTMAKER GO TO THE BATHROOM?

BECAUSE HIS BLOTTER WAS FULL.

Bedwetting Treatment According to Age

Child's Age (Years)	6–7	8–9	10 & Up
Education[1]	yes	yes	yes
Practical tips[2]	yes	yes	yes
Lifting[3]	yes	maybe	maybe
Pull-Ups at night[3]	yes	maybe	maybe
Calendar & praise[4]	yes	yes	yes
Bladder exercises			
• Water Gulping	yes	yes	yes
• Bladder Attention	yes	yes	yes
Waking Up Practice	yes	yes	yes
Bedwetting alarm[5]	maybe	yes	yes
Medication			
• Desmopressin	maybe	yes	yes
• Oxybutynin	maybe	yes	yes
• Imipramine[6]	no	no	maybe

Notes

1. Education means reading the first part of the book with your child and teaching her how her body works. Kids are usually interested in their bodies and love doing the balloon experiment in Chapter 2.

2. This refers to some of the basic things you do to make it easier to deal with wet beds, like sheet protectors and extra bedding (see Chapter 26).

3. I don't recommend lifting or Pull-Ups for older children except in special circumstances (see page 173 in Chapter 25).

4. Younger children may need help with their calendar, and they often prefer stickers instead of writing D after they've had a dry night.

5. Most children 7 years and older can understand the purpose for the alarm and, therefore, can accept its negative consequences, eg, getting woken up at night. A few 6-year-olds may be suitable candidates if they are highly motivated.

6. I don't use imipramine with children, but some doctors find it helpful for older patients who have not responded to other measures.

Appendices

Appendix

Waking Up Dry Checklist

Day of the Week	Sunday	Monday	Tuesday	Wednesday	Thursday	Friday	Saturday
Month & Date	___	___	___	___	___	___	___
Water Gulping	☐	☐	☐	☐	☐	☐	☐
	☐	☐	☐	☐	☐	☐	☐
Bladder Attention	☐	☐	☐	☐	☐	☐	☐
	☐	☐	☐	☐	☐	☐	☐
	☐	☐	☐	☐	☐	☐	☐
	☐	☐	☐	☐	☐	☐	☐
Waking Up Practice	☐	☐	☐	☐	☐	☐	☐

Every time you do one of your exercises, mark the appropriate box. If you're unable to fill out the checklist during the day, record what you did before you go to sleep at night. Permission to photocopy granted.

Health Screening Questionnaire

1. Has your child ever had a bladder or
   kidney infection? ☐ Yes ☐ No

2. Does your child complain of pain or burning
   when urinating? ☐ Yes ☐ No

3. Does your child urinate more than 9 times a day? ☐ Yes ☐ No

4. Does your child hold back urine for extended
   periods of time (ie, more than 8 hours)? ☐ Yes ☐ No

5. Does your child have daytime wetting accidents?
   (This includes having damp underpants
   throughout the day.) ☐ Yes ☐ No

6. Has your child recently begun wetting the bed
   after 6 months or more of being dry at night? ☐ Yes ☐ No

7. Does your child have trouble with his urinary
   stream? (This includes dribbling, a weak stream,
   or having to push hard to start urination.) ☐ Yes ☐ No

8. Does your child have damp underpants after
   going to the bathroom? ☐ Yes ☐ No

9. Does your child wake up more than once a
   night to drink water? ☐ Yes ☐ No

10. Does your child have a problem with abdominal
    pain or chronic diarrhea? ☐ Yes ☐ No

11. Does your child hold in bowel movements? ☐ Yes ☐ No

12. Does your child ever soil underpants with stool? ☐ Yes ☐ No

13. Has your child experienced a recent history of
    mood swings or other emotional problems? ☐ Yes ☐ No

14. Does your child snore heavily at night in such
    a way that your child sometimes stops breathing
    or struggles to breathe? ☐ Yes ☐ No

15. Does your child have insomnia, sleepwalking, or
    night terrors? ☐ Yes ☐ No

If you answered "Yes" to any of these questions, do not begin the
program without seeing your doctor or nurse practitioner.

Bedwetting Questionnaire

I included this questionnaire in case you decide to do the Waking Up Dry Program with your doctor or nurse practitioner. These questions explore your wetting history and those parts of your life that may affect the program.

There are a lot of questions, so it's okay to ask your coaches for help. They can fill out the form for you, and they can answer any questions you're not sure of. (The questionnaire your coaches filled out to check for medical causes of bedwetting is in Appendix B. Bring both questionnaires to your visit.)

1. Date

   _____

2. Your name

   _____

3. Your age

   _____

4. What grade are you in?

   _____

5. What is your teacher's name? (If you have more than one teacher, write the name of the one you like best.)

_____

6. What are your favorite subjects at school? (You can't pick recess!)

_____

7. Are you having any difficulties at school that might interfere with your staying focused on the program?   ☐ Yes   ☐ No

8. If you answered "yes," what are they?

_____

_____

_____

9. What are your favorite hobbies?

_____

10. What are your favorite sports?

_____

11. Name one of your heroes or someone you look up to.

_____

12. Has anyone in your family had to work hard to overcome a problem in his or her life?   ☐ Yes   ☐ No

13. If you answered "yes," who was it and what did they overcome?

_____

_____

14. Do you live in a house or an apartment?

_____

15. If you live in an apartment, do your next-door ☐ Yes ☐ No
    neighbors have children?

16. Is it possible that your neighbors would hear ☐ Yes ☐ No
    the bedwetting alarm if it goes off at night?

17. Do you have your own bedroom? ☐ Yes ☐ No

18. If you have to share a bedroom, whom do you share it with?

_____

19. Do you sleep in a bunk bed? ☐ Yes ☐ No

20. Is your bedroom located near your parent's ☐ Yes ☐ No
    bedroom?

21. If you answered "no," where is your bedroom located?

_____

22. Is your bedroom located near a bathroom? ☐ Yes ☐ No

23. If you answered "no," where is the bathroom located?

_____

24. Do you have carpeting in your bedroom? ☐ Yes ☐ No

25. Do you have carpeting in the hallway that leads ☐ Yes ☐ No
    to the bathroom?

26. Do you use a night-light or other light when you ☐ Yes ☐ No
    go to sleep at night?

27. Has anyone in your family ever wet the bed? ☐ Yes ☐ No
    (This includes parents, grandparents, siblings,
    and aunts and uncles.)

28. If you answered "yes," who was it?

_____

29. Does anyone outside of the family know that   ☐ Yes   ☐ No
    you wet the bed?

30. If you answered "yes," who is it and what is his or her
    relationship to you?

    _____

31. Is there anything that your friends or family   ☐ Yes   ☐ No
    have done about your bedwetting that has
    bothered you? (For example, teasing you or
    threatening to tell people that you wet the bed.)

32. If you answered "yes," what happened?

    _____

    _____

    _____

33. Have your parents restricted you in any way   ☐ Yes   ☐ No
    because of your bedwetting? (For example, not
    buying you a new mattress or sleeping bag.)

34. If you answered "yes," what happened?

    _____

35. Have you ever been punished for wetting   ☐ Yes   ☐ No
    the bed?

36. If you answered "yes," describe the punishment.

    _____

    _____

    _____

37. Do your parents both agree about your doing   ☐ Yes   ☐ No
    the Waking Up Dry Program?

38. Is there any stress going on at home that may make it harder for your parents to work on the program with you? ☐ Yes ☐ No

39. If you answered "yes," describe the problem.

_____

_____

_____

40. Are your parents separated or divorced? ☐ Yes ☐ No

41. If you answered "yes," how well do your parents communicate with each other?
    a. They communicate well about most issues.
    b. They communicate well if it involves their children.
    c. They don't communicate well about anything.

42. Is anyone in your family very sick or scheduled to have surgery in the next 2 months? ☐ Yes ☐ No

43. If you answered "yes," describe what's happening.

_____

_____

44. Do you have any brothers or sisters? ☐ Yes ☐ No

45. Is your brother or sister having any problems at home or school that might interfere with your working on the program? ☐ Yes ☐ No

46. If you answered "yes," describe the problem.

_____

_____

_____

47. Are you and your parents currently having any   ☐ Yes   ☐ No
problems like arguing a lot about homework
or family rules?

48. If you answered "yes," what are the problems?

_____

_____

_____

49. Are your parents planning to have or adopt a   ☐ Yes   ☐ No
baby in the next 2 months?

50. Are you planning to move or go on vacation in   ☐ Yes   ☐ No
the next 2 months?

51. Do your parents ask you not to drink after dinner ☐ Yes   ☐ No
to help you stay dry?

52. If you answered "yes," how much does this help?
    a. Not at all
    b. A little
    c. A lot

53. Have you tried anything in the past to treat   ☐ Yes   ☐ No
your bedwetting?

54. If you answered "yes," write down what you did and whether
it helped.

_____

_____

_____

55. Were you ever dry at night for more than   ☐ Yes   ☐ No
6 months in a row?

56. How often do you wet the bed?
    a. Less than once per week
    b. One to 2 times per week
    c. Three to 4 times per week
    d. Five to 7 times per week

57. How many times do you wet the bed at night?
    a. Once
    b. Twice
    c. Three times
    d. Unsure

58. Do your parents have an idea of the times when   ☐ Yes   ☐ No
    you usually wet the bed?

59. If you answered "yes," what times do you wet the bed?

    _____

60. When you wet the bed at night, do you go back to sleep
    in your own bed or do you get in bed with someone else?

    _____

61. Have you ever wet someone else's bed after   ☐ Yes   ☐ No
    wetting your own?

62. If you answered "yes," whose bed did you wet?

    _____

63. Do you ever wake up on your own to go to   ☐ Yes   ☐ No
    the bathroom?

64. If you answered "yes," how often do you wake up?
    a. Occasionally
    b. Frequently
    c. Always

65. Are you a deep sleeper?   ☐ Yes   ☐ No

66. If you answered "yes," how hard is it for your parents to wake you up?
    a. Not too hard
    b. Pretty hard
    c. Impossible

67. Do you ever wake up at night after you wet the bed? ☐ Yes ☐ No

68. If you answered "yes," how often do you wake up?
    a. Occasionally
    b. Frequently
    c. Always

69. Do your parents take you to the bathroom after you go to sleep? ☐ Yes ☐ No

70. If you answered "yes," how many times do they get you up?
    a. Once
    b. Twice
    c. Three times

71. If your parents take you to the bathroom, how often does this keep you dry?
    a. Always
    b. Sometimes
    c. Never

72. Are you dry if you sleep at a relative's house? ☐ Yes ☐ No

73. Do you wear Pull-Ups to bed? ☐ Yes ☐ No

74. If you answered "yes," when do you wear them?
    a. All the time
    b. On special occasions like sleepovers and vacations
    c. If you are sick
    d. _____

75. Do you avoid going on sleepovers because you're wet at night? ☐ Yes ☐ No

76. If you go on sleepovers, how do you handle your bedwetting?
    a. Wear a Pull-Up.
    b. Tell your friend about the problem.
    c. Have someone take you to the bathroom in the middle of the night.
    d. _____

77. Do you take any responsibility for cleaning up   ☐ Yes   ☐ No
    in the morning after having a wet bed?

78. If you answered "yes," what responsibilities do you take?

    _____

    _____

    _____

79. Do you pee during the day more than   ☐ Yes   ☐ No
    your friends?

80. Does it seem like you often run to the bathroom   ☐ Yes   ☐ No
    at the last minute to pee?

81. If you had to pee while you were riding in the car with your
    parents and you wouldn't be home for 15 minutes, what would
    you do?
    a. Hold back your urine with ease.
    b. Hold back your urine with difficulty.
    c. Ask your parents to pull over so you don't have an accident.
    d. _____

82. How much do you want to be dry at night?
    a. A little
    b. A lot
    c. More than anything

83. What's the best thing that will happen when you become dry at night?

_____

_____

_____

_____

_____

_____

Glossary

Alarm Clock Test: A method for determining if children can wake up at night, with or without their parents' help, in response to an alarm sound. If a child is able to wake up, he is a good candidate for the bedwetting alarm.

Arousal disorder: A medical term used to describe people who are "deep sleepers." Individuals with this condition have difficulty waking from sleep in response to internal or external stimuli, eg, sounds, touch, a full bladder.

Bedwetting: See *Enuresis.*

Bedwetting alarm: A device that teaches children to become dry at night. The alarm consists of a wetness sensor that goes in a child's underpants and an alarm unit that buzzes and/or vibrates when a child wets the bed at night.

Bladder: A muscular pouch that stores urine until a person is ready to urinate.

Bladder Attention: One of the bladder exercises used in the Waking Up Dry Program. It teaches a child to be more aware of the signals her bladder sends prior to urination.

Bladder capacity: The amount of urine the bladder can hold. Children who urinate frequently or have urgency before they urinate often have a small functional bladder capacity.

Constipation: The passage of large, hard stools. Constipation and infrequent defecation can cause daytime and nighttime wetting.

Deep sleep: See *Arousal disorder.*

Defecation: The process of passing feces out of the body.

Desmopressin: A manufactured form of vasopressin. Desmopressin treats bedwetting by reducing the amount of urine a child produces at night.

Dry-Bed Homework: A series of tasks that children carry out to determine if they are motivated enough to work on becoming dry at night.

Dysuria: A stinging or burning sensation that occurs during urination.

Encopresis: Fecal soiling in a child older than 4 years. It is usually the result of stool withholding in a child with chronic constipation.

Enuresis: The medical term for involuntary wetting in a child older than 5 years that is not caused by anatomic or neurologic disorders. If a child wets the bed at night, it is called *nocturnal enuresis.* If a child wets during the day, it is called *diurnal enuresis.* A child has *primary enuresis* if he never had 6 months of consistent dryness. A child has *secondary enuresis* if he had 6 months of consistent dryness and then began wetting again.

Enuresis alarm: The medical term for the bedwetting alarm.

Fecal impaction: A large, hard plug of stool in the rectum. This can cause abdominal pain, fecal soiling, and enuresis.

Feces: Solid waste that is eliminated from the intestinal tract.

Frequency: The sensation of needing to urinate frequently.

Hesitancy: Difficulty starting urination. This can occur because of the pain associated with a urinary tract infection or because a child has a voiding dysfunction.

Hormone: A chemical the body produces to regulate certain physiologic processes. Examples include thyroid hormone, growth hormone, and vasopressin.

Hypnosis: A technique that uses visualization, imagery, and posthypnotic suggestions to help people lose weight or stop smoking. Hypnosis can also be used to help children become dry at night.

Imipramine: A medication used by some doctors to treat bedwetting.

Incontinence: Involuntary wetting that is caused by an anatomic abnormality or neurologic condition.

Kidney: The organ responsible for eliminating excess water and certain waste products from the body.

Laxative: A medication used to treat constipation. Laxatives stimulate the intestinal tract to work harder to "push" feces through the body.

Lifting: The process of taking a child to the bathroom late in the evening to urinate. Parents typically do this before they go to bed themselves to prevent bedwetting episodes from occurring.

Nocturnal polyuria: The medical term used to describe excessive urine production at night. This occurs in children who don't make enough vasopressin.

Odor eliminators: Products that neutralize unpleasant odors.

Overactive bladder: When a bladder fills with urine, it normally accommodates the increased volume without a sudden rise in pressure. An overactive bladder is unable to do this, which leads to uncontrolled bladder contractions and a sense of urgency and frequency in affected individuals.

Overlearning: A technique used in conjunction with the bedwetting alarm to reduce the chances that a child will relapse after a bed-wetting program is complete.

Oxybutynin: A medication that relaxes bladder muscles. It is usually given to relieve symptoms such as urgency, frequency, and daytime wetting.

Pediatric nephrologist: A pediatrician that specializes in diseases of the kidney.

Pediatric urologist: A pediatric surgeon that specializes in diseases of the urinary tract. Pediatric urologists are experts at managing bedwetting.

Pelvic floor muscles: A group of muscles that supports the pelvic organs. The urethra and rectum pass through the pelvic floor.

Physicians' Desk Reference: A compendium of information on drugs and therapeutic agents used to treat medical disorders.

Pituitary gland: This is the master gland of the body's endocrine system. It is located at the base of the brain. (The *endocrine system* is a collection of glands that control certain physiologic processes through the release of hormones.)

Rectum: The last part of the large intestine. When feces collect in this area, a signal is sent to the brain alerting a person that it is time to defecate.

Sphincter muscle: The muscle that encircles the urethra as it exits the bladder. This is the muscle a person squeezes to hold back urination or stop the urinary stream when voiding.

Stool softener: A medication used to soften feces so they move through the intestinal tract more easily.

Underpads: Disposable or reusable products that can be placed on a bed to protect the mattress from urine.

Ureter: A small tube that drains urine from the kidney to the bladder.

Urethra: The tube that carries urine from the bladder out of the body. In males, it passes through the pelvic floor into the penis. In females, it passes through the pelvic floor and terminates in an opening right above the vagina.

Urgency: The sensation of needing to urinate very soon.

Urinary tract: The system of organs responsible for the production and removal of urine from the body—kidney, ureter, bladder, and urethra.

Urinary tract infection: A bacterial infection of the urinary tract. These infections can occur anywhere from the kidney to the bladder.

Vasopressin: A hormone secreted by the pituitary gland that reduces the amount of urine produced at night. Some children wet the bed because they do not make enough of this hormone.

Voiding: To void means "to empty." Doctors use the word voiding to describe the act of urinating.

Voiding schedule: If a child has daytime wetting because of uncontrolled bladder contractions or because she doesn't "feel" her bladder signals, a timed voiding schedule will often keep her dry. This involves going to the bathroom at regular intervals, usually every 2 hours.

Wake-up Drill: A technique used to help children wake up in response to the bedwetting alarm.

Waking Up Dry Calendar: The record children use to track their progress as they do the Waking Up Dry Program.

Waking Up Dry Contract: The contract children and coaches sign at the beginning of the Waking Up Dry Program. It ensures that everyone knows what is expected during the program.

Waking Up Practice: One of the behavioral components of the Waking Up Dry Program. Before children go to sleep at night, they lay in bed and practice getting up to go to the bathroom. This teaches them to go to the bathroom if they need to urinate during the night.

Water Gulping: One of the bladder exercises used in the Waking Up Dry Program. By drinking more during the day, children get more practice going to the bathroom. This regulates their voiding pattern and makes it more likely that they will respond to their bladders at night.

Tips for Cheerleaders

If you're reading this section, it means you were selected to be a cheerleader for someone who is doing the Waking Up Dry Program. I wrote this section to let you know what responsibilities go with this important job.

Bedwetting is a common condition that affects more than 5 million children in the United States. Because children do not talk about bedwetting outside the family, most of them think they are the only ones with this problem. Bedwetting is rarely caused by a serious medical disorder. In most cases, a child wets the bed because of a combination of being a deep sleeper and having a small bladder. Children do not wet the bed on purpose.

Learning to become dry takes a lot of work. The most effective treatment for bedwetting is a device called the bedwetting alarm. Most bedwetting alarms are small, battery-operated devices that children wear to bed at night. One part of the alarm attaches to their undershirt or pajama top and the other part attaches to their underpants. When the child urinates, the alarm goes off, creating a loud buzzing sound. The sound is designed to wake the child up and teach her what her bladder feels like when it fills up with urine. As the alarm begins to work, it teaches children to wake up before they wet the bed. Interestingly, by the time the program ends, most children sleep through the night because their bladders have learned to hold all of their urine until morning.

Because the alarm wakes children up night after night, they may become tired or frustrated while they're waiting for progress. (It can take up to 4 months before a child becomes dry using the alarm.) When I'm working with children in my office, I have 2 jobs. My first job is to teach them how to use the alarm. My second job is to cheer them on. Although family members are as excited as I am when their children start having dry nights, I like to call my patients on the phone to let them know I'm proud of them and that I'm pleased with how hard they're working. I came up with the cheerleader idea because I can't take on this role for kids who are using this book.

The bedwetting alarm is only one part of the Waking Up Dry Program. Here is a brief summary of the other parts:

- **Waking Up Dry Calendar.** Children use this to record wet and dry nights and monitor their progress.

- **Waking Up Practice.** This is an exercise that helps children learn to wake up at night to urinate.

- **Bladder exercises.** The program has 2 exercises designed to increase bladder size and a child's bladder awareness.

- **Weekly rewards.** Children get small rewards once a week for cooperating with the program.

- **Special reward.** Children get a large reward after they have completed the program successfully. This reward is like a graduation present for a job well done.

It would be impractical to repeat everything that's in the book in one or two pages. If you'd like more familiarity with the program, you can ask the child's coaches or pick up a copy of the book.

Here Are the Things I Would Like You to Do During the Program

1. Call the night before the program begins to wish the child good luck.

2. Call 2 days into the program to see how things are going.

3. Talk with the child once a week until he's dry.

4. Be supportive.

5. Encourage the child to report his progress.

6. Listen to the child if he feels like complaining about the program.

7. Listen to the child if he feels like complaining that his progress is slower than he wants it to be.

8. Tell the child what a good job he's doing.

9. Don't push too hard if the child doesn't feel like talking about the program on any particular day.

10. Remind the child that by practicing and sticking with the program, his chances of becoming dry are excellent.

Here Are Some Examples of Phrases You Can Use

- I'm really proud of all the work you're doing to become dry at night.
- How is the program going?
- Is the program harder than you expected?
- You sound tired. Did the alarm wake you up last night?
- I hear that you woke up when your alarm went off last night. That's terrific!
- Tell me what you're proud of so far.
- I remember when I was a kid and I was learning how to _____. Some days went well and others didn't. It frustrated me at the time, but now I realize that people always have ups and downs when they're learning something new.
- Are things going the way you hoped they would?
- What reward are you getting this week?
- Does the program make it harder for you to get ready for school in the morning?
- I'm proud of you.

- Does _____ (the child's sibling) know about the program? Is he/she being helpful?
- Tell me what happened this week.
- Your coaches told me that you're cooperating with them. Keep up the good work.
- You were dry last night. That's great!
- You're doing a super job!
- You're really good at remembering to think about your bladder.
- What's the best thing that will happen when you're dry every night?

Tips for Doctors & Nurse Practitioners

Near the end of my internship, one of my attendings asked me if I planned on doing a fellowship. When I told him I was interested in primary care pediatrics, he gave me a word of advice: "If you're not going to specialize, find something that interests you and make it your own area of expertise. Then, years from now, you'll have this special interest to keep things exciting."

I thought about this advice for a few days and then, months later, recalled it vividly when I found myself getting interested in enuresis. In the years that followed, I read everything I could find on the topic and began to develop the protocol that became my Waking Up Dry Program.

I stated in the introduction that one of my motivations for writing this book was to give children a program they could use at home with their parents. But I also know from conversations with colleagues that the book can serve as a manual for health care professionals. In truth, I hope that most of the children who buy the book decide to use it with the support and encouragement of their doctors or nurse practitioners.

I also mentioned at the beginning of the book that practitioners might change some aspects of the program to fit their own approach to bedwetting. Nevertheless, I wrote this section to provide some additional information about the nuances of the program. I do not mean to be presumptuous, however, so please take the following information in the spirit in which it was intended.

How I Work With Children in the Office

I usually conduct my bedwetting consultations over two 1-hour visits. The first visit is informational—I make a tentative diagnosis, provide lots of details about the way the body works, and send the family home with instructions to evaluate the child's bowel and bladder habits. The second visit is treatment oriented—I assess the patient's motivation and build the program based on the child's individual needs. The book will enable you to accomplish this in much less time.

Children are usually embarrassed or self-conscious at bedwetting visits; therefore, I never start out asking them about their enuresis. I begin with a little small talk and then ask them lots of questions about their home, school, and hobbies. These questions not only let me ease into our bedwetting discussion, but they also provide valuable information about the child's world. For example, by watching how the child interacts with his parents, I get a sense of how well they communicate. By asking about the child's heroes, I learn about a person I can refer to later if the child gets discouraged and I need to discuss what it takes to stick with the program. Asking questions about a child's home environment lets me know if there are any physical obstacles that may affect the program. For example, it's harder to use the enuresis alarm if a child's parents sleep on a different floor in the house.

My main goal at the first visit is to teach children how their bodies work and let them know why they're wet at night. I inform them that millions of kids wet the bed and there is nothing wrong with them. (Obviously the specifics of this exchange are tailored to the child—if I have someone with daytime wetting or other problems, I alter what I say about their health.) I teach children how their nerves work, and we fill up balloons with water to see how the external sphincter muscle operates (sometimes they get wet by "accident"). I use a lot of repetition during the visit to make sure my patients understand what I'm teaching them, but I do so in an animated way and give them lots of positive feedback as we go along. If the child comes to the office with one parent, I ask him to "teach" the absent parent about the program that evening. I let him know that the parent who accompanied him to the office will help, but that he will be the one who does the teaching. This puts children in a position of authority, which they love.

When I give kids their Dry-Bed Homework at the end of the first visit, I do it in a constructive manner. I often say something like, "Peter, you did a great job today. You really listened to what I had to say, and you learned a lot about your body. Remember that I'm the coach of the Waking Up Dry Team and you're still trying out for the squad. I have some homework for you to do so you can show me how much you want to be on the team. This homework is important because it gives me some information I need for the program and tells me if you're ready to become dry at night. However, from today's visit, I'm sure you are." At the end of the visit, I let the kids know that their parents will be my assistant coaches and they will help out with the homework. This approach works very well for children between the ages of 6 and 10 years. For older kids, I tone things down, but communicate the same message.

If I sense some indifference on the child's part, I playact with him. Most of the time, I extend the sports example by pretending that I'm the one who's trying out for the team. I act a little silly and use a whiny voice as I say things like, "Oh, man, I'm tired. I don't feel like practicing today." After a few moments, I ask the child how a coach would feel if a player behaved this way. I usually hear that the coach wouldn't like it. I then ask if a player is likely to make the team with this attitude. I usually hear that the player wouldn't make the team. I do all of this with an enthusiastic tone, guiding the child to the correct answers if necessary. By the end of the exchange, most kids are smiling and showing me the eagerness I like to see. I then tell them to go home and blast through their homework. I also remind them that they will be scoring goals in no time! (I adjust this comment based on the child's favorite sport or hobby.)

When kids come back for their second visit, I can tell fairly quickly how well I "reeled them in" at our first meeting. For example, if a child forgets his calendar or didn't do all of his homework, this usually means that he's not motivated enough to do the program. It's important to recognize, however, that kids have different temperaments, and quiet or introverted children may be more tentative during all phases of treatment.

The most important part of the second visit is determining if the child is ready for the enuresis alarm (see Chapter 11). If a child is not ready for the alarm, I suggest some simple behavioral measures to address the wetting. In many cases, this is all that's needed to help a child become dry at night. If a child is ready for the alarm, we set up the program at this visit. This includes reviewing the various exercises the child will do and going over the Waking Up Dry Contract. Because I want children to feel some degree of ownership of what we're doing, I let them make some decisions about which elements we incorporate into the program.

I repeatedly emphasize that the child is the star of the show, but that he will also be the one does the most work. (This is a good time to mention how much work his hero did to become a winner.) I want children to realize that the more involved they are with the program, the more likely it is that they will succeed. A comment I often make is, "Are you going to let your bladder be in charge of you, or are you going to be in charge of your bladder?"

It's important to practice certain parts of the program in the office—for the child and so parents can see the right way to do things. This is especially true for Waking Up Practice and the enuresis alarm. I show kids some of the alarms described in Chapter 17 (we review their pros and cons) and let them choose the one they like best. Because it's impractical for you to buy this many alarms, you can request brochures for these products or keep a few models on hand to show patients.

I always rehearse the correct and incorrect way to respond to a buzzing alarm. The first time I set off the alarm, the child pretends to be so sleepy that he doesn't wake up. This gives the parents a chance to practice the Wake-up Drill. The second time I set off the alarm, the child wakes up quickly, turns off the alarm, and pretends to pee in the bathroom. At the end of the visit, we review the program and I ask if there are any questions. I then tell the child that he's now part of the Waking Up Dry Team and I think he's going to do a great job. Even though it will take a lot of work, I remind him that his head coach and assistant coaches are here to help and, in time, he will become the boss of his body!

The most important thing to do at the beginning of the program is to give children positive feedback while they're still having lots of wet nights. To accomplish this, I call the family on a regular basis once the program begins. If a patient starts the program on a Friday night, I call the following Monday and weekly thereafter until steady progress is being made. I schedule additional office visits as needed, but always want families to know that I'm available to answer questions and fine-tune the program.

Although I avoid medication with most patients, there are 2 circumstances in which the alarm itself may not be enough to help a child overcome his wetting: (1) if a child is wetting multiple times per night, or (2) if a child is making very little progress 4 to 6 weeks into the program. Desmopressin is most likely to be effective in children with nocturnal polyuria who have a normal bladder capacity. Oxybutynin is most likely to be effective in children with a small bladder who set off their alarms multiple times per night.

Before I use medication with this group of patients, I have parents take them to the bathroom around 11:00 pm to try and reduce the number of wettings per night. If this doesn't work, I add a medication to the program. Once a child has been dry for 14 consecutive nights, I wean the lifting or medication over a 2- to 4-week period, adjusting my timing according to their clinical response.

The Waking Up Dry Program

Now that I've discussed my approach to bedwetting, let's review some rough numbers for the program. If a child passes the Alarm Clock Test, her chances of quitting are much lower than the 25% described in the literature—fewer than 10% of my patients drop out of treatment. My success rate for getting kids dry is also better than what is quoted in the literature (85% vs 50%–75%). The following 3 things contribute to this success:

- The program attacks bedwetting from different angles.
- I eliminate less motivated children before we start.
- I'm not dealing with a referral population, which may contain a higher percentage of children who are difficult to treat.

Approximately 15% of my patients relapse after becoming dry. Most all of these patients become dry if they repeat the program.

Most children who quit the program do so because they aren't having the progress they hoped for or the program turned out to be harder than they expected. When this happens, I praise the child for his cooperation and comment on any aspect of the program that went well. I then ask if there is any part of the program that he would like to continue. If he says "yes," I adjust the program accordingly, hoping to add other elements in the future. If the child isn't interested in continuing with the program, I tell him that's okay. The important thing is to minimize negative feelings about the program because that will make it more difficult for him to try again in the future.

Periodically, I see patients who tried really hard to become dry, but nothing worked or provided lasting results. When this happens, I tell the child I'm proud of the effort he made, but that his body isn't cooperating with the program. I usually suggest that he take a break and try again in 6 to 12 months. In the interim, I recommend a scheduled lifting program, with 1 or 2 awakenings per night, to try and keep him dry. Another option in this situation is desmopressin. The *Physicians' Desk Reference* recommends using desmopressin for up to 6 months, though recent research suggests it's safe to use for longer periods.[1] If you prescribe desmopressin for more than 6 months, you should stop the medication every few months to see if the child still needs it. Finally, a small group of children require a combination of desmopressin and oxybutynin to attain nighttime dryness.[2]

I hope this information is useful and the book is a handy reference for teaching your patients to become dry at night.

References

1. Wolfish NM, Barkin J, Gorodzinsky F, Schwarz R. The Canadian Enuresis Study and Evaluation—short- and long-term safety and efficacy of an oral desmopressin preparation. *Scandinavian Journal of Urology and Nephrology.* 2003;37:22–27
2. Nevéus T. Oxybutynin, desmopressin and enuresis. *Journal of Urology.* 2001;166:2459–2462

Supplemental Reading

Bedwetting Alarm

Bradbury M. Combination therapy for nocturnal enuresis with desmopressin and an alarm device. *Scandinavian Journal of Urology and Nephrology Supplement.* 1997;183:61–63

Butler RJ. Combination therapy for nocturnal enuresis. *Scandinavian Journal of Urology and Nephrology.* 2001;35:364–369

Butler RJ, Robinson JC. Alarm treatment for childhood nocturnal enuresis: an investigation of within-treatment variables. *Scandinavian Journal of Urology and Nephrology.* 2002;36:268–272

Hvistendahl GM, Kamperis K, Rawashdeh YF, Rittig S, Djurhuus JC. The effect of alarm treatment on the functional bladder capacity in children with monosymptomatic nocturnal enuresis. *Journal of Urology.* 2004;171:2611–2614

Bladder Mechanics

De Wachter S, Vermandel A, De Moerloose K, Wyndaele JJ. Value of increase in bladder capacity in treatment of refractory monosymptomatic nocturnal enuresis in children. *Urology.* 2002;60:1090–1094

Kawauchi A, Tanaka Y, Naito Y, et al. Bladder capacity at the time of enuresis. *Urology.* 2003;61:1016–1018

Medication

Bennett HJ. Imipramine and enuresis: never forget its dangers. *Pediatrics*. 1982;69:831–832

Butler RJ, Holland P, Robinson J. Examination of the structured withdrawal program to prevent relapse of nocturnal enuresis. *Journal of Urology*. 2001;166:2463–2466

Butler RJ, Robinson JC, Holland P, Doherty-Williams D. Investigating the three systems approach to complex childhood nocturnal enuresis—medical treatment interventions. *Scandinavian Journal of Urology and Nephrology*. 2004;38:117–121

Kruse S, Hellström AL, Hanson E, Hjalmas K, Sillen U, for the Swedish Enuresis Trial (SWEET) Group. Treatment of primary monosymptomatic nocturnal enuresis with desmopressin: predictive factors. *BJU International*. 2001;88:572–576

Robson WL, Norgaard JP, Leung AK. Hyponatremia in patients with nocturnal enuresis treated with DDAVP. *European Journal of Pediatrics*. 1996;155:959–962

Rushton HG, Belman AB, Zaontz MR, Skoog SJ, Sihelnik S. The influence of small functional bladder capacity and other predictors on the response to desmopressin in the management of monosymptomatic nocturnal enuresis. *Journal of Urology*. 1996;156:651–655

Miscellaneous Topics

Austin PF, Ritchey ML. Dysfunctional voiding. *Pediatrics in Review*. 2000;21:336–341

Egger J, Carter CH, Soothill JF, Wilson J. Effect of diet treatment on enuresis in children with migraine or hyperkinetic behavior. *Clinical Pediatrics*. 1992;31:302–307

El-Anany FG, Maghraby HA, Shaker SE, Abdel-Moneim AM. Primary nocturnal enuresis: a new approach to conditioning treatment. *Urology*. 1999;53:405–409

Honjo H, Kawauchi A, Ukimura O, Soh J, Mizutani Y, Miki T. Treatment of monosymptomatic nocturnal enuresis by acupuncture: a preliminary study. *International Journal of Urology*. 2002;9:672–676

Landgraf JM, Abidari J, Cilento BG, Cooper CS, Schulman SL, Ortenberg J. Coping, commitment, and attitude: quantifying the everyday burden of enuresis on children and their families. *Pediatrics*. 2004;113:334–344

Longstaffe S, Moffatt ME, Whalen JC. Behavioral and self-concept changes after six months of enuresis treatment: a randomized, controlled trial. *Pediatrics*. 2000;105:935–940

Nappo S, Del Gado R, Chiozza ML, Biraghi M, Ferrara P, Caione P. Nocturnal enuresis in the adolescent: a neglected problem. *BJU International*. 2002;90:912–917

Olness K. The use of self-hypnosis in the treatment of childhood nocturnal enuresis. A report on forty patients. *Clinical Pediatrics*. 1975;14:273–275, 278–279

O'Regan S, Yazbeck S, Hamberger B, Schick E. Constipation a commonly unrecognized cause of enuresis. *American Journal of Diseases of Children*. 1986;140:260–261

Robson WL. Diurnal enuresis. *Pediatrics in Review*. 1997;18:407–412

Robson WL, Jackson HP, Blackhurst D, Leung AK. Enuresis in children with attention-deficit hyperactivity disorder. *Southern Medical Journal*. 1997;90:503–505

Van Kampen M, Bogaert G, Akinwuntan EA, Claessen L, Van Poppel H, De Weerdt W. Long-term efficacy and predictive factors of full spectrum therapy for nocturnal enuresis. *Journal of Urology*. 2004;171:2599–2602

von Gontard A, Schaumburg H, Hollman E, Eiberg H, Rittig S. The genetics of enuresis: a review. *Journal of Urology*. 2001; 166:2438–2443

Review Articles

Hjalmas K, Arnold T, Bower W, et al. Nocturnal enuresis: an international evidence based management strategy. *Journal of Urology.* 2004;171:2545–2561

Jalkut MW, Lerman SE, Churchill BM. Enuresis. *Pediatric Clinics of North America.* 2001;48:1461–1488

Lawless MR, McElderry DH. Nocturnal enuresis: current concepts. *Pediatrics in Review.* 2001;22:399–407

Nevéus T, Läckgren G, Tuvemo T, Hetta J, Hjalmas K, Stenberg A. Enuresis—background and treatment. *Scandinavian Journal of Urology and Nephrology Supplement.* 2000;206:1–44

Schmitt BD. Nocturnal enuresis. *Pediatrics in Review.* 1997;18: 183–191

Thiedke CC. Nocturnal enuresis. *American Family Physician.* 2003; 67:1499–1506

Sleep

Nevéus T. The role of sleep and arousal in nocturnal enuresis. *Acta Paediatrica.* 2003;92:1118–1123

Wolfish NM. Sleep/arousal and enuresis subtypes. *Journal of Urology.* 2001;166:2444–2447

Index

C